Discipline Your Thoughts

Uncover The Origins of Your Thoughts, Correct Common Thinking Errors, and Critically and Logically Assess Your Beliefs

By Steven Schuster

stevenschusterbooks@gmail.com

www.stevenschusterbooks.com

everyone. This work is sold with the understanding that the author is not engaged in rendering medical, legal or other professional advice or services. If professional assistance is required, the services of a competent professional person should be sought. The author shall not be liable for damages arising herefrom. The fact that an individual, organization of website is referred to in this work as a citation and/or potential source of further information does not mean that the author endorses the information the individual, organization to website may provide or recommendations they/it may make. Further, readers should be aware that Internet websites listed in this work might have changed or disappeared between when this work was written and when it is read.

For general information on the products and services or to obtain technical support, please contact the author.

Table of Contents

Introduction 9

Part 1 23

Chapter 1: A Primer 25

Chapter 2: Become the Critique of Your Own Thinking 41

Part 2 51

Chapter 3: Decision-Making, Belief, and Behavioral Biases 53

Chapter 4: Anchoring 61

Chapter 5: Availability Heuristic 73

Chapter 6: Bandwagon Effect 81

Chapter 7: Confirmation Bias 89

Chapter 8: Empathy Gap 99

Part 3 113

Chapter 10: Social Biases 115

Chapter 11: Authority Bias 121

Chapter 12: False Consensus Effect 129

Chapter 13: Illusory Superiority 137

Chapter 14: Ingroup Bias 147

Part 4 155

Chapter 15: Memory Errors and Biases 157

Chapter 16: Egocentric Bias 163

Chapter 17: Illusion of Truth Effect 175

Final Thoughts 183

Reference 187

Endnotes 199

Introduction

To err is human and, I, for one, can attest to that. Whether we are expecting the worst to happen or are certain we know what others must be thinking, our brains are hardwired to think in certain ways. While the brain is truly exceptional, it isn't perfect or infallible. The human brain often makes the same kinds of errors that as a matter of fact are highly predictable.[i] Learning about these thinking errors can help us identify them easier and live with them in a more conscious and cautious manner.

You've probably spent most of your adult life feeling sure of yourself when it comes to how your mind works. You likely feel secure in your ability to make decisions without being influenced by any outside forces and are sure that you know why you think certain things. Let's test this theory. Take a moment to create a picture in your mind of a lucky dwarf. I know, it sounds a very random thing to think about. Still, please do think of a lucky dwarf. Did you do it?

Now think of a number from one to ten. Don't overthink it. Just go with the very first number that pops into your mind. Do you have your number?

I'll bet you were thinking of the number seven. My guess may be wrong, but on average, 95% of people choose the number seven after they are requested to think of a lucky dwarf.[ii]

Don't worry, I'm not a mind reader, and I did not just pull a long-distance Jedi trick on you. Rest assured, this book will provide you with answers about why you almost certainly thought of the number seven, how I knew you probably would, and much more.

How and why do people typically choose the number seven after hearing or reading the words "lucky" and "dwarf"? Our brain has a semantic network, a cluster of all the information we have learned over time. Each concept in our brain network is connected to other concepts that are related in some way. Because of this connection, whenever a concept in our semantic network gets activated through some kind of *priming*—in our case, my word priming with "lucky" and "dwarf"—all of the other concepts related get activated too. According to Collins and Loftus in their work *A Spreading Activation Theory of Semantic Processing*[iii], we call this phenomenon "spreading activation."

If we apply the spreading activation theory to our lucky dwarfs, we realize that we have connections with the phrase "lucky number seven," or "Snow White and the Seven Dwarfs."

Since these concepts are connected in our mind, dwarf—seven—lucky, when one of them gets activated, the others get activated too—on a subconscious level. And when you have to make a snap decision about them, like choosing the first number that pops into your mind, it is likely you will choose the number that your mind delivers the easiest.

I'm sure when you chose a number, you were convinced that you chose that number by your own free will. What about now? Are you still sure?

As you can imagine, this is not the most powerful example of mind priming out there. All commercials and sales rely on priming the mind of the consumer. Understanding how our mind can be influenced, how it falls into subconscious biases and how to detect these can be a real asset. This book will talk about similar mind tricks and their effects on our everyday lives.

In economy, it is assumed that people behave in a rational manner and that's how they make their financial decisions. Behavioral economics has a different approach. Behavioral economics distances itself from making any judgment without empirical evidence so first just looks at how people behave. Experts of this field make research in labs and in real life, in the field to see how people behave and draw their consequences. Thanks to the observations made by behavioral economists it became clear that the behavior of people often proves to be more irrational than traditional economics suggests.

There is one way to be rational and many ways to be irrational. Think about emotions: if you were in a forest 2000 years ago and you saw a wolf pack how do you think that as a human being you would behave? Would you pause to think, to analyze the situation, calculate what you should do, what are the costs and benefits and risks of certain actions? Of course not. You would run the moment you saw the wolves.

That's how emotions work. When we see something that puts us in danger, or when we encounter ourselves in a situation where attraction is involved we turn our cognition off. We don't think. We just feel and execute the command our brains give us. In the case of the wolf situation, you only heard the command run; you didn't think, didn't calculate, just ran.

Emotions work the same way today as they did hundreds or thousands of years ago. Although we don't often encounter a pack of wolves on a casual Friday night, there are other things that trigger us; a sales advertisement, someone cutting in front of us on the road, someone upsets us, we have the same emotion-driven reactions as our ancestors.

Don't get discouraged. Just because we have this tendency it doesn't mean that we can't improve their impact on our lives. There is hope to help ourselves in these situations. This book is talking about these hopes in detail.

My hope is that after reading this book when you see something you will be able to identify it as an emotional hijacking or a thinking error and will be able to fix it.

Let's see some common thinking errors of today. For example, think about the magic word *free*. Most people are going for free stuff even if they don't need it or if it is not good for them. But it turns out that if it wasn't free, we wouldn't have the same lure to it. Ask yourself whenever the temptation of free bamboozles you if you'd buy that thing if it cost a dollar?

People have the tendency to observe easily the irrationalities in other people. When others are exhibiting irrationalities people often think that they don't behave so irrationally. That they are rational *above average*. Studies proved that more than seventy percent of people think they are above average, better than their peers. Something must be wrong with math here. Or is something wrong with our objectivity? Behavioral economist and professor of psychology, Dan Ariely, suggests that the best thing we can do when noticing irrationalities in our peers is to use our observations as a mirror. Did your friend make an irrational shopping decision? I'm sure you made some too in your lifetime. Did your brother fall for the wrong girl again? You made some wild decisions in the name of love too. Instead of wasting your thought on how your fellow humans are more irrational than you it is better to think of strategies on how to prevent the detected irrationality in your life.

Becoming aware of an irrational decision—regardless who does it—and brainstorming solutions of how to prevent them in the future is the first step to becoming more rational and making better decisions.

Another way to prevent making mistakes is practicing things that we could do that would avoid the situation. How many times do you enter a restaurant when on a diet and, while pledging to eat only a salad, the waiter ends up serving you a double cheeseburger with fries? You tell yourself "just today." Sure enough, no one is innocent in this mental blooper. Or were you pledging to get yourself a better helmet for the next motorbike season but when the moment comes and you sit on your bike, this pledge doesn't seem so important anymore because you can't imagine getting into an accident?

I understand neither of these cases is something that you can fix at the moment. You probably won't send back the cheeseburger or call an Uber instead of finally having a free ride. You won't be like "let me fix these cognitive errors." In these situations it is especially crucial to think before we even engage in irrational behavior and try to prevent ourselves from doing them in the first place.

This requires a lot of practice, of course. But also requires you to know your irrationalities well, think ahead, and force yourself to do something before you'd engage in the irrational behavior that makes it impossible to fall prey. For example, if you know that you need to lose weight but you hate going to the gym and dieting, schedule appointments with a personal trainer or friend beforehand who will force you to do those push-ups. Or you can ask the waiter to, instead of bringing the menu, just tell you what kind of salads they have so you don't even see the other options.

What I have been talking about until now is behavioral economics in action. What is behavioral economics more precisely?

This field of science is a blend of psychology and economics that aims to provide information about how and why people are *not* behaving in their best interests. Behavioral economics gives the framework to understand when and how we make cognitive mistakes. Some of these errors are quite predictable because they occur in specific circumstances. Other errors can happen in a nonspecific nature, we can expect them to happen nevertheless. Behavioral economics aims to create solutions that help people to make wiser, better decisions to enrich their lives.

Behavioral economics was a response to the rational choice model promoted by traditional economics. Originated from Adam Smith, the rational choice model claims that people are acting in their best interest, carefully weighing the costs and benefits of their decisions. Allowing people to act on their best decision will create a just, free, self-sustaining market. Adam Smith, however, didn't assess human behavior correctly. People are fairly often not sure of their preferences and, sometimes, frankly don't even know what and why they are thinking. Traditional economists assumed that people have great self-control, laser-sharp awareness about the long-term benefits of their decisions, they can delay gratification for a greater reward. Contemporary psychology proved that this is simply not the case.

Behavioral economists realize and accept that people have limited control over their cognitive abilities, their willpower is limited, their self-control easily wavers, and the decisions they make are often about instant gratification than long-term wellbeing. The human mind is greatly influenced by the context of a presentation, by emotions, and the preferences of others.

Daniel Kahneman, psychologist and Nobel Prize winner in economics, had the following remark, "it seems that traditional economics and behavioral economics are describing two different species."

Behavioral economics sheds light on human irrationalities, why we self-sabotage, can't keep our self-control, fall into the same mental traps over and over again. Neuroscientists argue that the human brain is composed of different parts, each following its own logic. There is no dominant decision maker among these parts. Because of these multiple decision makers are we sometimes sabotaging ourselves? We can have seeking pleasure and avoiding pain as our main goal, we might not always make the best decisions to achieve them.[iv]

Behavioral economics integrates a psychological understanding of human behavior into economic analysis. This field of science runs parallel with cognitive psychology, trying to guide people toward healthier behaviors by correcting cognitive and emotional errors to the pursuit of real self-interest.[v]

We are hard-wired to make thinking errors and often we need a reminder to make decisions in our best interest. To do this we need to understand where we go wrong and how can we manage our lives better. This book will help you to navigate your mental life more smoothly. I can't promise that by the time you finish reading this book you will be free of thinking errors—that would be a thinking error on my side. Or worse, a big, fat lie. No, you can't change how your mind works. But you can change your reactions. You can detect, recognize, and overwrite your thinking hiccups closely after they happen. Closely enough to be able to not react on them impulsively or not make a poor decision as a consequence.

Without further ado, please open your mind and join me to discover the greatest roller coaster of your life called a brain.

Part 1

General Laws to Discipline Your Thoughts

Chapter 1: A Primer

Mental discipline is not something that you can achieve by a good night sleep or a few motivational quotes on the internet. Training your mind to be objective is a long, grueling process. Bad thinking habits, cognitive biases, and stress play vital roles in hindering your ability to think healthy. Because these things cause your mind to just be reactive to everything, they prevent you from having control on your thoughts.

Every day, we are faced with various situations that may bring out the toxicity of our minds.

Traffic jams, cranky customer, pressure—these things can easily become our triggers. Most people tend to just avoid situations like these, but they fail to realize that it's not the situation that should be changed. It's how they react to it.

Before we move on to the ways we can discipline our mind, it is important that we first identify the bad thinking habits that we commonly subscribe to. Below are some questions that I need you to answer truthfully:

- Do you make excuses when you make a mistake?
- Do you avoid confrontations?
- Do you easily jump to conclusions?
- Have you ever felt the need to distance yourself from a person who criticized you?
- Does your mind unconsciously focus on the negative side of things no matter what you do? [vi]

If your answers are mostly yes, then it is clear that your brain needs a reboot to change the way it processes your thoughts.

Most people do not realize the power of their own thoughts. They fail to notice that thoughts can literally shape their world and the way they see it. When they engage in dysfunctional thinking practices, they are practically setting themselves up to their own demise. When an unhealthy mind takes over, the quality of life that they can potentially have is undermined.

In this chapter, you will learn different ways to overturn the bad habits of your own mind. With continuous practice, you will be able to see a big difference in how you react to things around you, how you arrive at a decision and, ultimately, how you manage your emotions.

The CAR Technique

The Catch—Accept—Replace[vii] technique is an effective tool that you can practice when it comes to cognitive bias avoidance. When you consciously make an effort to stop yourself from falling into unhelpful thinking habits again, a disciplined mind is formed sooner than you expect.

Catch Your Undisciplined Thoughts

The first step toward a strong mind is to acknowledge your vulnerability to harmful cognitive activities. It is inevitable to experience times wherein your mind just succumbs to thoughts like illogical reasoning, prejudice, and hasty conclusions. The moment you acknowledge and admit to these bad habits, you are already one step closer to changing them.

Police your own thoughts.

Each individual responds differently to triggers. It is important that you are aware of your own warning signs. If you feel like stress is already creeping up your body, it is time to take a step back. Heightened awareness of your own frequency is the key.

I once had a colleague who just couldn't manage her own stress. She easily snapped and had a really short temper. Even the smallest things like a slow printer ruined her day. Needless to say, she made the people around her feel bad too by being constantly in a foul mood.

Since we were close, I straight up asked her if she was aware of her problem. Surprisingly, she said yes. She said she knew she was ill-tempered but could not really help it. She said her reactions were very automatic. She actively sought ways to fix her mood swings but she kept on falling back in.

That was when I realized that issues like short temper and other unhealthy thinking habits are not a result of a conscious choice. Sometimes it is because our minds get so accustomed to such routines that we fail to explore any other ways to cope.

I then introduced the CAR technique to my colleague. I asked her to list her warning signs and her red flags. From feelings of irritation to physical manifestations like curling her fists into a ball, we were able to identify her signals. That was the start.

She tried catching herself whenever she started feeling annoyed or clenching her fists. She knew this was her cue to step back and take a breath. Because she trained herself to be in tune with her unhealthy tendencies, with time she was able to gain control and prevent her mind from reacting harshly to stressful situations. She still sensed the stressful emotions rising but she knew that if she just took a few deep breaths and told herself, "this is not about me, this is not against me," she could react to her emotions in a calm, collected manner.

Being aware of your bad mental habits of handling strong emotions and catching yourself before reacting impulsively is definitely not an easy feat. It is a constant push and pull of reminding yourself, again and again, overcoming emotions, and trying different prevention strategies. But once you get used to it, keeping your mind under your own surveillance will not be as difficult and daunting.

Accept Your Emotions

Now that you know about the art of catching your own dysfunctional practices, it is of no use to keep on denying them or making excuses for your behavior. The next step to awareness is acceptance. You have to fully accept and take accountability for your own thoughts and emotions.

When faced with a difficult situation, it is human nature to look for something to put the blame onto.

We are always so desperate to escape stressful moments that we tend to point fingers and even find fault in the situation—but never in ourselves.

As mentioned, most of the time we feel bad, not because of the situation, but because of how we react to it. The way you handle your emotions speaks volumes on how you are going to overcome your problems. As cliché as it may sound, it really is mind over matter. You have the power over your own thoughts and feelings.

Ultimately, you have the power to change what needs to be changed.

Replace Your Habits

The most important thing in this training is your will to change your habits. If you claim to be aware of your harmful mental practices but not do anything about them, then nothing will improve.

You have to constantly find ways to change the content of your thinking and reactions.

I understand that in finding your own way of thinking, you might feel the fear of being too different from how other people think. I want you to know that it is okay. And also that you're the "victim" of some cognitive biases when you have thoughts like that. Take trait ascription bias for example. This is the tendency to view yourself as relatively different and colorful in terms of personality, behavior, and mood while seeing others as much more predictable. Another bias associated with thinking that you are significantly different from others is the illusion of asymmetric insight. Here you perceive your knowledge of your fellow humans to surpass your fellow humans' knowledge of you.[viii]

Assuming that you are much better at detecting cognitive biases than the crowd, it's another cognitive bias. This bias is called "bias blind spot" and refers to seeing ourselves as less biased than other people or to be able to identify more cognitive biases in others than in oneself.[ix]

Replacing your thoughts with positive ones is ideal, but certainly not always realistic. Not everyone can stay positive amidst tough calls. When I say replace your thinking habits, it does not mean that you only think of happy thoughts and never get stressed. No. What I mean is that you have to learn to be able to fully engage yourself with unfavorable emotions, notice and accept cognitive biases and yet manage to remain level-headed.

You will know that you have achieved such changes if you remain open despite criticisms; if you are able to understand and accept other people's shortcomings; or you do not let a spilled coffee ruin your day. There will be many moments in your life that will mark your progress. Take note of them. Take pride in them. At the end of the day, you will realize that changing your unhelpful thinking habits was one of the greatest decisions you have ever made in your life.

A disciplined mind creates a healthier, better, and freer life.

Using Meditation Techniques to Discipline Your Thoughts

Meditation is a technique that requires total mind conditioning. Focus and balance are required to achieve the clearest mental and emotional state. If you are in the process of training to discipline your mind, meditation is a good way to get started.

In this age of technology and fast-paced lives, our brains are wired to get stimulated by even the smallest and most random information. There is an abundance of information-prompting everywhere that tend to easily capture our attention. Our goal is to have the power to disengage and keep still amidst distractions.

Meditation is just the perfect tool for that.

Commitment

The moment you start exploring the benefits of meditation, you are starting a long-term commitment with yourself, for yourself. This is the commitment to a routine/schedule. Except for serious circumstances, you are expected to stick to your meditation practices despite a busy day or feeling under the weather.

Staying committed is easier if you have a strong personal reason for doing meditation in the first place. Your motivation is your drive.

Whatever your motivation may be, it is important that you keep going and you keep showing up. You will reap the benefits sooner than you know.

Consistency

Commitment comes with consistency. To achieve a disciplined mind, you need to develop a regular meditation schedule. This means that you practice meditation during the scheduled time no matter what. Meditation should not depend on your mood but your will.

Just like sports, you are disrupting your own progress by your inconsistencies. If you skip meditation from time to time, you will just find yourself going back to zero. Your consistent practice is vital in the development of your concentration, mindfulness, and receptive awareness.

Discipline

Self-discipline is the ability to filter productive and harmful thoughts. It allows you to act within reason instead of just acting by impulse. For a person who meditates, self-restraint is very important.

Self-restraint works on a lot of things. It could mean renouncing your fantasies or resistance to daydreaming. It means that you need to preoccupy your mind with the object of your meditation, may it be your breathing or a mantra.

However, it is important not to confuse discipline/self-restraint with repression. You don't want to be punitive on yourself when your mind unconsciously wanders off or when your brain weaves unhealthy thoughts again. Instead of pushing yourself to the edge, just let your thoughts flow freely. Let whatever thoughts arise, then slowly shift back to your object of meditation.

Meditation is a rigorous training for the mind. Your drive, environment, and tools will determine how much you can free yourself from active thinking.

If you keep on practicing meditation, you will be acquainted with its ins and outs and how it affects your mind. Each individual experiences different benefits. As long as you are following a regular meditation schedule, you will notice a difference with how you think and even behave. Coupled with exercises and yoga practices, you will even reap physical benefits as well.

Here is a quick recapitulation for how to set yourself swiftly up for meditation:

1.   Make sure you are in a peaceful environment. Your comfort is your priority.

2.   Close your eyes. You can use tools such as eye masks and special pillows. As you go along, you can even invest in a meditation chair.

3.   Breathe freely. Do not try to control it or follow a certain pattern.

4.   Lastly, choose an object of meditation. For beginners, it is usually your own breathing. Try to

focus on how you inhale/exhale. This will help you put your attention on a single thing and prevent your mind from wandering.

5.   It is normal for the mind to still go off despite your efforts to focus on one thing. Do not be bothered and just try to shift your focus back to your breath again.

Try meditating now for a few minutes. Good luck!

Chapter 2: Become the Critique of Your Own Thinking

I cannot stress enough how quality thoughts lead to a quality life. No matter who you are—a CEO, an employee, a mother, a friend—no one is exempt from the consequences of a poor mental state. As long as you do not realize the importance of skilled thinking, you will make bad decisions over and over again.

But how exactly do we achieve skilled thinking?

As confusing as it may sound, you have to think about the way you think. Skilled thinking does not come naturally. It is achieved through a serious study of how your mind works and how it manufactures thoughts. Just like a car, you have to make sure that you have read the manual before hitting the road. In case of any problems, you know which parts to fix and which tools to use.

Exploring the ins and outs of your mind is the first step in being the critique of your own thinking. You have to familiarize yourself with how your brain usually ticks when presented with various situations.

Are you in tune with your own mind? Ask yourself these questions:

- Have I ever evaluated myself when reacting to a stressful situation?
- Am I aware of my own thought process?
- Am I in touch with my own emotions? [x]

If your answers are no, then now is the perfect time for you to reassess your psychological habits. More often than not, we tend to think that our feelings, reactions, or thoughts should come out naturally all the time. While this belief may hold true to a certain degree, controlled thoughts and emotions are still the best tools in overcoming any situation. Life decisions are not about your moods, they are about how wisely you think. Splurting our every thought without previous consideration is not a sign of "being yourself," but rather of emotional immaturity.

1. Clarify your thinking.

Clarifying your thoughts means that you are on the lookout for any vague or formless thinking. Usually, formless thoughts come from not fully understanding something or someone. When this happens, it is best that you strip yourself of arrogance and acknowledge the truth that there are times when we will not understand something. And that's okay.

If you have someone you can consult, do not hesitate to ask for help. Have them repeat or explain their arguments or ask them to help you figure out the things you did not understand. Humility and honesty go a long way.

When you still don't understand someone's point, you can ask them to kindly provide you examples. This will help you relate it to something closer to you or your experiences. Personalizing ideas is the best way to comprehend them fully.

If you think you have understood well enough, practice summarizing thoughts with your own words. This will help you test your comprehension about something. As Albert Einstein said, if you can't explain it simply, you don't understand it well enough. You can use statements or expressions such as I think, in other words, here are my two cents about it, etc.

Clarifying your thinking means that you look beyond the surface. You try to figure out the real meaning of things instead of putting your own interpretation to it. With this practice, you can avoid misunderstandings due to misinformed opinions. Only after you become fully informed about something can you form an opinion about it. Remember the golden rule:

Never agree nor disagree with anything someone says until you fully understand them.

2. Question Questions.

Critical thinkers do not only know how to ask questions but also know what types of questions to ask. They do not settle for half-truths or simply agree to anything that is presented to them. They ask. They probe. They also listen carefully to other people's questions.

To become a critical thinker, you have to examine the extent to which you are a questioner, or how you accept the definition of things. Do you simply agree to avoid confrontations? Do you scrutinize things until you are satisfied?

A skilled mind knows how and when to ask questions. This is to effectively deal with the world around you. You can ask a question of clarification or validation. You can formulate questions to avoid cognitive biases. Just know that when you question something, make sure that it is of relevance and weight.

You cannot simply throw in questions because you want to. Questions need to be thought out too.

How do I question my questions? Here are some samples:

- Will the answer to this question help solve the issue at hand?
- Is my question free of any bias?
- Is there another way to look at their point of view?
- Am I genuinely curious or am I just throwing some loaded questions?
- Are there more important questions that I should be asking instead of this one? [xi]

Policing your own questions allows you to avoid seeming superficial or even ignorant. When someone has a disciplined mind, he knows that even questions have to be of quality as well.

3. Be Reasonable.

As I have mentioned, humility and honesty go a long way. If you want to train your mind, you have to tame your ego. Realize it is impossible to always be right. There will always be bad days when your views are just plain wrong.

The last and most important step to being the critique of your own thinking is to be reasonable. Reason moves mountains. When you do not deal with things with proper reasoning, then you can expect that you will always face a lot of issues.

In any situation, you always have to respect other people's opinion. When engaged in a heated argument, step back and look at the bigger picture.

Be reasonable enough to consider if what he says has merit. Do not rob other people of the opportunity to be right.

When you find yourself unwilling to listen to other people or becoming defensive, take a break. Try to analyze why you are behaving that way. Is it because they don't get your point? Is it because they are misinformed? No matter what your reason is, avoid losing your temper by immediately identifying what is irking you in the situation. Then try to address it.

Conversely, when you think other people are being unreasonable, politely call them out. The sad truth is that most people have a hard time changing their minds once set. Still, try putting reason into them.

Calm and collected thinkers are those who understand that their quality of thoughts lies in their knowledge about how the mind works. They do not only recognize its importance but actually put in some effort to study the mind and its behavior. Then they use this knowledge and apply what they learn to the different situations they face. No matter how mundane, they know how to maneuver around any life situation. All thanks to a disciplined mind, these thinkers know how to maximize their life's potential because they know how to make the best decisions.

Part 2

How to Get a Grip On Your Behavioral Biases?

Chapter 3: Decision-Making, Belief, and Behavioral Biases

We'd all like to think that we approach the world with a completely sober mind, but often this is simply not the case. We journey through life carrying our own personal sets of biases with us. It may be a preconceived notion or just a stubbornness to believe what we want to believe without really taking other opinions or evidence into account. Wherever the bias comes from, the result is the same. These biases can help form our beliefs and impact nearly every aspect of our lives. From the economic and business decisions we make to the way we behave in our daily lives; our biases cause us to react to specific situations in a way that is different from the way we would like to behave.

As human beings, our similarities far outnumber our differences. Our biases are no exception. There are many common biases that impact our decision-making, beliefs, and behavior. Here are some quick examples:

- Are you a dog mom or dad? Do you buy your pets birthday presents, talk to them when they greet you at the door after a hard day at work, and consider them to be a part of your family? If so, you, like me, may be exhibiting *anthropomorphism or personification bias*. This is the tendency to assign human traits and feelings to animals and other objects. I often feel that my dog understands me better than other human beings just because he so patiently and intently stares at me when I talk to him. He doesn't interrupt me, and after I'm done with my confession he climbs up into my lap and lets me pet him without any sign of self-interest—or so I believe. If this scenario sounds familiar to you, you may be guilty of anthropomorphism. While it may seem an innocent bias, in severe cases people can get to a point where they depend too much on the objects of their anthropomorphism while ignoring their real relationships.

Anthropomorphism is a very common phenomenon in literature and child stories. Think of all the Disney movies where the main characters were animals, the Andersen tales, or the Egyptian gods. We have a natural tendency to give human attributes to non-humans.[xii]

Personification bias dresses more abstract concepts in human traits like a nation, an emotion, or the seasons.

- *Conjunction fallacy* is people's tendency to make predictions based on the assumption that specific conditions are more likely to occur than more general ones. For example, if you see an old friend from high school who loved to cook when you knew her, seeing on social media that she attends college, human nature would make you more inclined to assume that she attends college for culinary courses rather than assuming that she attends a college for any other field of study.

- *Gamblers fallacy* is the faulty belief that the chance of an outcome happening in the future is impacted by things that have happened in the past when really, the probability hasn't changed at all. For example, if you are flipping a coin and it has repeatedly turned up tails, you may think that it is due to turn up heads next. In reality, the probability of a coin landing on heads is always one out of two, no matter how many times you flip the coin or what the coin lands on in previous flips.

- *Hindsight bias* is the "I always knew it would turn out that way" line of thinking. The problem is that the prediction comes a bit too late as the event has already happened. We are always smarter after something happens. It's only natural, right?

- The *framing effect* is looking at the same information and making different judgments simply based on how the information was presented. Is the glass half full or half empty? Do you save twenty percent of the price or pay eighty percent of the price? Which sounds more attractive? In the case of positive framing, saving twenty percent, the deal sounds tempting. You immediately start debating buying that product. If the same deal is portrayed negatively, stressing its costs, you might not buy the product.

- *Functional fixedness* is the bias that prevents you from thinking outside the box. It is when you are mentally stuck and can only use an object in the way it has always been used before. It was a typical habit of my grandma, may she rest in peace, that she resisted every kind of innovation. "In our day it was done like this and it was done well," was her argument every time.

These cognitive biases exist in all of us. They are a part of human nature. The more we are aware of these tendencies within us, the more we will be prepared to address and overcome them when they impact our decision-making, beliefs, and behavior in ways that may not be beneficial to us.

In the following chapters, I will discuss some of the most common behavioral biases in detail. These biases are:

- anchoring,

- availability heuristics,

- bandwagon effect,

- confirmation bias,

- empathy gap.

Chapter 4: Anchoring

What is Anchoring?

Just as a boat relies on an anchor to hold it in place, our brains often rely on anchors. However, our mental anchors don't always work to our benefit. Anchoring, also known as imprinting or focalism, is the tendency to rely too much on the first information we saw or heard regarding a specific situation as we try to make decisions. Often, the first thing we learn about a topic is not the best information we could use. Once an anchor is set in our mind, we go on to use it as the standard to which we compare other similar things.

We become biased as we interpret other information that arises as wrong if it doesn't coincide with the initial information we had. For example, if we have a price for a refrigerator acting as an anchor in our mind, prices of other refrigerators we look at which are lower than that price will seem like a very good deal to us, even if the price is still higher than what the refrigerator is really worth.[xiii]

Konrad Lorenz conducted an experiment with geese that helped him to discover the theory of imprinting—anchoring—in 1935. In his experiment, he separated newborn goslings into two groups—one that would see their mother goose first after birth, as is usually true with geese, and one that would see him first after birth. The goslings followed whichever large moving object they saw first, whether it was the mother goose or Lorenz, since their instincts told them they needed to in order to get food and protection, and ultimately, to survive.[xiv]

Goslings imprint upon the first moving things they see. Do we humans tend to do the same—not at birth, but when we encounter new information on a topic? According to studies and research, yes. Let's see some examples.

Imprinting often happens to us when we shop. We can get imprinted on a price tag, or a specific product and its price tag. I discovered this firsthand when I was shopping for a new dining table. I really liked it but I found the price quite high. I decided to look further to find the right table but every time I looked at another table, I found myself thinking back to the price of the first dining table I really liked. When I saw something that was cheaper, I started rationalizing that I didn't really like it, besides if I just put X dollars to this table's price, I could get my favorite table. When I found a table with a higher price tag than the one I anchored on, I felt a sudden urge to go back and get the original one—which at this point didn't seem so expensive anymore.

Can you guess which table I got? Based on my story, you would say that I got the first table, my first choice. Don't fall into conjunction fallacy, my friend. Of course, my wife chose the table in the end.

A similar story can be told for so many purchasing decisions people make. Prices become imprinted in our minds and act as anchors for everything from produce at the grocery store to big-ticket items like cars and houses.

Try to recall what anchoring price you attach to some products you often buy? How much is bread supposed to cost? Or milk? How do you feel about a price rise? If you usually paid $2 for milk how would you feel if tomorrow it cost $3?

I must confess to often having an internal outrage when I go to the grocery store and see that my favorite products rose in price. Heaven forbid I start comparing these prices to the prices they had twenty years ago. Then I tend to become vocal about my outrage. When this happens, my daughter just shakes her head disapprovingly, saying, "Dad, you've become old." Ouch.

How does anchoring affect your life?

When we see the original price on a price tag with a twenty percent off sale occurring, we feel like we are getting an amazing deal. We no longer consider the true worth of an item; the original price listed has now become the anchor in our minds, and we are happily willing to pay the sale price just because it is less than the initial price. If we buy a house for less than the list price, we are thrilled, thinking that we were excellent negotiators, even though the true information we should have been studying to make an unbiased decision is the fair market value and the prices of comparable homes in the area, not just the anchor of the list price.

Anchoring extends far beyond purchasing decisions. As you could see with the case of the table and me, anchoring can happen to be products, fashion choices, restaurant choices, food that you find acceptable, and so on. I have many friends who are pizza lovers and not particularly picky about it, but ever since they visited Italy, and had pizza there, no American pizza seems to satisfy their new anchor for pizza. That's right. We can get anchored to something we already know but we discover a superior option.

We also have the tendency to change our anchor regarding price. For example, if your goal is to buy the cheapest bread you may be faithful to a bakery only until you discover another one where the bread is even cheaper. You'll adjust your anchor to the new price and comparatively the bread you bought before will seem like a bad deal. Depends on what's important to you. If you seek the best quality bread, price will be irrelevant. You'll change your anchor once you find a bread that you like more than the one you had before.

Anchoring can manifest itself in abstract life expectations. A dear friend of mine was diagnosed with COPD—chronic obstructive pulmonary disease—sixteen years ago. When she received her diagnosis, she did some research and found out that the average survival rate for someone with similar health concerns was eight years. Now as she reaches the end stages of her disease, she feels quite content thinking that she has "beaten the odds" and lived longer than expected. Her anchor is quite different than that of her children, who saw their grandparents live to be in their eighties and were hoping their mother would do the same.

How do we "fix" anchoring?

Often, we make decisions thinking that they are a one-time choice without realizing that they may continue to impact many of our choices far into the future. We have seen that in many ways, we act as the goslings did with Lorenz, holding onto the first piece of information we are presented with and allowing it to influence us.

It is important to step back and evaluate our initial decisions and understand why we made them.

Did we make them because we did our research and made a wise decision in the first place, or did we stumble upon them randomly without realizing that those decisions can quickly turn into long-term habits?

We need to examine how we came to choose our career, our friends, our clothing and hairstyle, and so many other things to see if we need to re-evaluate our choices based on new information, or if we can stand by the original choices because they were truly good for us.

Consider if you choose to frequent a restaurant because you have sampled the menu and you really like the food that is offered at a reasonable price, or if you go there simply because the parking lot is full, so you assume it must be a great place to eat. Do you upgrade to the latest smartphone because you have compared the features of several brands and determined that the new phone best meets your needs, or is it because you have always upgraded to the latest edition of that brand of phone every few years, and that's just what you do?

You might come to find that many of your decisions are made out of habit and could benefit from you taking a second look at why you made them in the first place.

Anchoring itself doesn't necessarily have to be a bad thing. Here are a few tips to use anchoring to your potential benefit.

1.) Acknowledge your anchors. Ask yourself questions that could reveal anchoring behavior. If you're trying to decide whether to sell or hold onto your property, are you considering this choice on the information you know right now about the real estate market, or are you basing your selling price on what your neighbors say, a friend who just bought a house, or other factors that may be less relevant to the real estate market's future course?

2.) Create your own anchor—and be ready to modify it if needed: Anchoring can be helpful as long as it is suitable for your situation. It is crucial to set your anchor based on your needs and goals. For example, if you want to sell your property quickly because you need money for an urgent medical intervention, you shouldn't price the property on the higher end of its market price. It may be difficult to sell it quickly with a spicy price tag. If your circumstances change, be ready to modify the anchor. For example, if a relative can lend you the money for your medical intervention, you can raise the property's price a bit higher to not lose too much—or even make money on the sale.

For example, one of the most important decisions in a person's life is his or her expected retirement date.

The same concept is applicable to retirement. Anchoring your retirement age based on when your dad retired isn't the wisest choice because his situation, retirement age limit, health condition may have been completely different from yours. A better approach is to look at a representative, larger sample, like the typical age employees retire in your work field, and then adjust this number based on your own case.

When choosing an anchor voluntarily, stay flexible. The more you'll learn about the situation you anchored, it's reasonable to assume that the decision should be revisited occasionally to make sure it's in line with what the new knowledge is telling you.

3.) Take a look on history: Let's say you're trying to choose a tool to invest in. A good way to do this is to anchor on the historical growth rate for the tool in question—let's say stock market and 2% growth—then adjust your anchor from that percentage according to your beliefs on how the future will unfold derived from historical facts.

You can try to set an anchor on how much you estimate you'll spend monthly when you retire. It could be a good start to set the anchor around the amount you're spending now. Then think about what you would like to do in your retirement—travel more, stay at home more, start a new hobby, etc. Assess which costs may fall out from your everyday spending, and what new costs should be considered. Then adjust your anchor based on this information.

Chapter 5: Availability Heuristic

What is availability heuristic?

Availability heuristic is our tendency to overestimate how likely events are to occur that have a greater "availability" to us in our memories. Events can be more available to us in our memories based on how recently they occurred, how unusual they were, or how strong emotions were connected to the memories. This is a bias in which we base our present decisions and judgments on past ideas and information that immediately pop into our mind.

Let's test your availability heuristic sensors. Which job do you consider being more dangerous—being a cop or a logger? While the news talks much more about police shootings, statistics actually show that loggers are more likely to die doing their job than police officers.

Do you fear to hop in your car going to visit your friend? Not likely. Do you murmur a prayer each time you hop on a plane to visit a friend? More likely. Americans have a 1 in 114 chance of dying in a car crash, according to the National Safety Council. The odds of dying in air and space transport incidents, which include private flights and air taxis, are 1 in 9,821.[xv] In purely statistical terms, it's more dangerous to drive a car than to fly on a plane.

When it comes to making a judgment about relative risk or danger, the brain relies on mental shortcuts that help make fast, but often incorrect assessments. Availability heuristic is a common mental shortcut relying on information that comes to mind quickly and easily. If you can quickly think of more than one example of something happening—such as airplane crashes or police shootings—you will think they are more common than they actually are.

We tend to think that if we can remember something that must make it more important than other ideas we can't easily remember.

If we remember an event and its consequences, we tend to perceive those consequences to be unavoidable and we believe they are likely to continue again in the future. Anytime we can easily remember multiple examples that are similar to one another, it further cements their importance in our mind as something we can trust as we make a decision, because we think they are likely to happen again in the future.[xvi]

How does availability heuristic affect your life?

At times, we take our memories and use them to make connections between things that aren't really similar. Sometimes our ease in recalling something distorts our accurate estimates of its frequency, likelihood, and normalcy.

Take, for example, watching the coverage of a hurricane on television. People are exposed to prolonged coverage in vivid detail which will make a strong impression on their minds. They may come to assume because they are able to readily recall information and images about the hurricane, that area of the world is far less safe than it really is, and that future hurricanes are more likely to happen there. In reality, munching too much sugar is a much greater everyday danger worldwide. It claims more lives than hurricanes but it is much less likely to receive the extensive coverage by the news media. Thus we are less likely to readily recall all of the recent information on diabetes. The same is true of watching the nightly news broadcast. After it is over, you may go to double check your front door being locked thinking that crimes are much more prevalent than they really are. Why? Because that is the most recent information you were presented with.

In business, investors often use only the latest information that they can recall or their own lasting feeling about the economy to drive their decisions about whether they should invest or not. They are less likely to study multiple sources of information or history, long-range market performance, and forecasts, and as a result, may miss out on some good investment opportunities or take unnecessary risks.

In criminal justice, the availability heuristic can play a significant role. Some research studies asked people to give their opinion about the sentences being handed down by judges. The vast majority of people surveyed thought that judges were too lenient in issuing sentences. The same people were presented with examples of court cases, and after they studied them, decided to assign largely the same sentences that the judges had. Why the gap between their perception of the judges and agreeing with them in reality? Often, the cases that are covered by the media are violent and extreme. The more mundane and common cases do not receive the same attention. Because the people in the study could more readily remember the more violent cases, they incorrectly perceived the judges as being disproportionately lenient on crime, without considering what the average cases were. After the second survey, it turned out that they agreed with the decisions of the judges quite often.[xvii]

Another study assessed whether jurors perceive a witness to be more or less honest based on when they told a lie. The study revealed that if a witness told the truth at the beginning and then told a lie at the end, they were thought to be more dishonest than a witness who told a lie at the beginning and then told the truth at the end. This example shows the availability heuristic at work, as people tend to remember the latest information they can recall. If a witness tells the truth at the end, that is what the jurors remember better, so they perceive the witness as rather honest.

My cook friend once told me an insider secret about his restaurant. He was well aware that their food was mediocre to poor but they had excellent desserts they sold together with the main course as a meal. The reason? People usually evaluate based on their last impression. Thus having a good dessert could improve my friend's kitchen's questionable reputation. "They go away with a good taste in their mouth. That's what matters," he explained.

How to fix availability heuristic?

Try to catch yourself when you are making snap judgments. Daniel Kahneman in his book *Thinking, Fast and Slow*, points out that taking the time to think slowly in addition to our typical fast thinking can help. He believes we have two minds at work: the fast mind that makes snap judgments and the slow mind which is deliberate in its thinking and looks deeper into issues.[xviii]

Try this little exercise to use both your fast and slow mind. Ask yourself a question like, "Who is the most famous singer in the world?" Undoubtedly, your fast mind will jump in and make a snap decision to come up with an answer like Madonna, Michael Jackson, or Freddy Mercury. Once you have your snap answer, try to move beyond that. Ask yourself, "Who is the third-most famous singer in the world?" Now your slow and deliberate thinking mind will be activated as you dig deeper.

Keeping both minds at work will only serve to help you as you try to gather a more complete and accurate picture and make the most informed decision possible. Using your slow mind is the cure of availability heuristic because this practice is exactly about not using your gut-judgment and easily accessible ideas.

Chapter 6: Bandwagon Effect

What is bandwagon effect?

The bandwagon effect refers to people's tendency to do or believe things just because a lot of other people do too. It is related to groupthink or herd behavior.

They are often willing to ignore their own values, preferences, and beliefs just to go along with the crowd. The phrase originated from a bandwagon being used in a parade. It was a float that encouraged people to jump on and enjoy the music that was playing. It was often used in 19th-century political campaigns in an attempt to make candidates appear to be fun-loving and make people believe if they did not join in—and get on the bandwagon—they would be missing out on something great.[xix]

While the first time you ever heard of the bandwagon effect might have been when you were a child and your mother asked you, "If all of your friends jumped off a bridge, would you do it too?" you can probably think of a hundred more examples of the bandwagon effect.

Pop culture is a prime place to see the bandwagon effect in action. In 2012, there was a song released called "Gangnam Style." You undoubtedly heard of it as it became quite the music and dance phenomenon all around the world. YouTube and social media helped to spread the craze even faster as nearly everyone seemed to become an overnight fan; this is the epitome of the bandwagon effect.

Another example of the bandwagon effect was on display around the holidays in 1996. A little toy called Tickle Me Elmo became an overnight craze and was in such high demand that people were trampled in stores by shoppers trying to purchase limited supplies. It is hard to believe that a giggling Sesame Street toy could possibly become as instantly popular as it was without people being wired to the bandwagon effect. A toy which retailed for $29.99 was being offered for sale at prices of up to $10,000 because the demand came to far exceed the supply that holiday season.

How does it affect you?

The bandwagon effect goes far beyond purchasing and political decisions. It probably has had a much greater impact on your life than you realize. People tend to connect their beliefs and actions with a group, which is sometimes referred to in psychology and sociology as "herd mentality" or "groupthink." We would like to think that when we are making decisions they root in of our free will, rather than following the crowd. This can be true in some cases but we also need to increase our awareness of the instances when the bandwagon effect tries to sneak into our lives.

We tend to adopt the behaviors that we see in those around us, so choosing to surround ourselves with people who make positive, healthy choices is very important. If we are around people who read a lot, we are likely to spend more time reading too. If our colleagues, friends, and family members are politically active and aware, it is more likely that we will be too. If the people we spend the most time with eat healthily and exercise, we probably will too. If we are around happy couples and families, the chances are greater that we will be willing to put in the hard work—and have picked up some good skills from watching them—that it takes to make our relationships happy and successful too.

Unfortunately, the bandwagon effect can lead us to follow the dark side too. If you are raised in a family where you eat to show affection and not just when you are hungry, the likelihood that you may struggle with your weight in adulthood increases. If you grow up seeing dysfunction in relationships like lying, infidelity, abuse, or neglect, you will likely have to work harder to overcome those tendencies in your own adult relationships.

If you surround yourself with people who don't subscribe to the philosophy that you should never settle for less than your best, you might fall into that same mindset. You may start to give up and resign yourself to thinking that you don't deserve anything better than the current circumstances you are in. You might not set the high expectations for yourself that will help you break the cycle of negativity and achieve what you really want in life.

When voting in elections, the bandwagon effect is at work when people are greatly impacted by poll results. Their vote may often be cast based on who is expected to be the winner because they want to feel like they voted for the winning side. This influence tends to be strongest for people with a weak political party affiliation, or none at all.

In sports, the bandwagon effect is quite common. It often happens when an underdog team begins to perform better than expected. Many people who were never fans before suddenly join the growing group supporting the team. There may be a significant increase in team jerseys and merchandise being sold as more people join the bandwagon. Any new Croatia fans, soccer lovers?

How to fix the bandwagon effect?

Critical thinking is the best deterrent to blindly following the group. When we are aware of how easily we can fall into the bandwagon effect, we need to be willing to question ourselves and our decision-making process. If we pause to examine whether we are frequenting a restaurant because we really like the food, or simply because we get influenced by the queue in front of it, we are taking the first steps toward the kind of self-awareness that will help us combat the bandwagon effect and make better individual decisions.

Ask yourself the following question:

- If nobody… (queued here) would I still choose to… (eat here)?
- If no one… (listened to this music), would I still like it?
- Am I really a person who loves this, hates that, does this, says that…?

Asking powerful questions that bring our self-awareness to our true values can help us break the influence of the bandwagon effect. To succeed for real with a positive taste in our mouth, we also need to be ready to tolerate the displeasure of the crowd. Being different often means the majority won't agree with us. This can be challenging because we fear becoming an outcast. But if your friends are truly your friends and your friendship is more important than your personal opinion of basketball teams, political inclinations, they will accept you. They might tease you but that only gives a new flavor to your friendship.

Realize that most of the areas where bandwagon effect is present are not life-or-death questions. They are just opinions. Normally opinion differences shouldn't affect healthy, adult relationships. You can rest assured that just by following your own heart instead of the common opinion won't harm your closest relationships.

Chapter 7: Confirmation Bias

What is confirmation bias?

People believe what they want to believe. It is in our nature to seek out information that supports our beliefs and ignore information that does not. When we actively try to seek information that contradicts our preconceived ideas, we may find that it feels unnatural and difficult to do so. It takes effort and work on our part. Warren Buffet said, "What the human being is best at doing is interpreting all new information so that their prior conclusions remain intact."

Think about a belief you have. It can be any belief; religious, political, scientific, or personal. Try to recall a time when someone questioned your belief. What was your first instinct? Recalling all the data that supports your belief. When you ran out of your own reasons, you automatically started researching news, studies, information that confirms your belief instead of disproves it. This is a very human thing to do but can lead to a lot of headache in society.

Confirmation bias is also known as "myside bias" or "confirmatory bias." Confirmation bias is strongest in those beliefs we really hold dear. Because of this bias, it is completely possible for two people with opposing views to look at exactly the same information and draw entirely different conclusions to support their individual viewpoints.[xx]

There is a difference between a desire to be right and a desire to have been right. A desire to be right will lead us to seek the truth and have a hunger for knowledge, but if we discover that we were wrong we accept it. A desire to have been right will make us stubbornly hold onto our beliefs, even when we're presented with information that disproves them. It doesn't allow for us to admit we were mistaken, and it keeps us stuck in a rut and unable to advance our knowledge.

In order to conserve some of our mental energy, our brains rely on shortcuts and habits. Constantly evaluating and adjusting our view of the world as new information becomes available takes a lot of work and energy. Our brains often fall back on shortcuts to save time when making decisions and to keep from getting overwhelmed. When we find information that confirms our beliefs, we are comforted by how easy it is and how little mental energy it takes.

How does confirmation bias affect us?

When we fail to examine information in an unbiased fashion, we run the risk of making significant miscalculations. It is important for us to learn to identify confirmation bias in others and ourselves so we can work to overcome this thinking error. We can't overcome it if we are not aware of it.

Confirmation bias gives us a distorted view of information and muddies our judgment. It is similar to availability bias in that we tend to remember information that supports our beliefs. We may have a selective memory in that we remember what we want to.

Why do we ignore contradicting evidence? In our fast-paced world, we are under a constant barrage of information. Our brains have to figure out how to interpret, store, and retrieve that information when we need it. It is easier for our brain to focus on one idea at a time so it seeks to strengthen our view of the world, rather than constantly challenge and change it. We embrace information that confirms our beliefs and take it seriously, while we are inherently skeptical of information that goes against them. All of this causes our beliefs to become further entrenched.

Jennifer Lerner and Philip Tetlock found through their research that we are usually only inspired to think critically when others hold us accountable. If we need to justify our actions and beliefs to other people, we will look beyond evidence that merely confirms them. We don't want others to think we think we aren't logical, so we are willing to put in the extra effort. If we side with the beliefs of others, we can feel more connected socially.[xxi]

Examples of Confirmation Bias in Action

Social Media

The very nature of our social media feeds is a demonstration of confirmation bias in a tangible way. Things that we like on social media lead to similar topics and ideas being sent to us, which solidify rather than challenge our opinions. In times of political elections, the confirmation bias on social media is off the charts, as people repost articles they like and agree with and dismiss, disagree with, or respond angrily to those that don't support their views. This causes our political opinions to become even further entrenched. This bias can cause people to be unwilling to listen to or respect the opinions of those who disagree with them. There are many stories of people who unfriended those they cared about on social media because things became too emotionally charged.

Scientific Experiments

Neil deGrasse Tyson said, "One of the biggest problems with the world today is that we have large groups of people who will accept whatever they hear on the grapevine, just because it suits their worldview—not because it is actually true or because they have evidence to support it. The striking thing is that it would not take much effort to establish validity in most of these cases… but people prefer reassurance to research."

When I would get my students ready for the science fair, the hardest thing for them to accept was the idea that it was perfectly fine for them to prove their hypothesis wrong. They always wanted to change their hypothesis at the end to make it fit the data or to keep trying their experiment over and over again until they got the results they wanted.

In any good scientific experiment, the goal should always be for the researcher to disprove their hypothesis rather than confirm it. But as scientists are human, they are subject to falling prey to the same biases as everyone else. Sometimes their bias distorts their interpretation of the data, drives them to repeat the experiments until they get their desired result, or makes them more likely to give a positive peer review to studies that confirm their own views.

This causes a problem because it can lead to research supporting hypotheses which are simply untrue. Confirmation bias can waste time and money that is critical to important research. We have to be cautious about taking anything at face value and be aware that bias can be anywhere.

How to fix confirmation bias?

This chapter can be a good place to start questioning your own confirmation bias. Ask yourself:

- Which parts did I instantly agree with?
- Which parts did I ignore or glance over without even thinking about them?
- How did I react to ideas I agreed or disagreed with?
- Did this chapter confirm any ideas I already had? Why?
- What if I believed the opposite of those ideas?

Stop reading further and answer these questions. What did you conclude? I agree to disagree so feel free to be skeptical of my words. Do you notice you disagree? That's fine. But now please, for the sake of practice, try to find reasons why your disagreement could be wrong and try to find paths which could lead you to agree. Did you agree with me? Thank you. But now I challenge you to disagree with me. Try to imagine yourself as someone who thinks that what I said is total bollocks. Try to find the reasons and pathways that would make someone disagree with me.

You can take this exercise to the next level. Turn on your television and, regardless of your political views, start watching the opposing party's channels. Try to stay calm when you hear something that you disagree with. Simply notice that, "yes, I can sense my disagreement. Now I will make a conscious effort to find three reasons why could people agree with this statement." And do it. It will be quite difficult at first but the more you practice it, the easier it will be to understand opposing views. You don't have to agree with them. That's not the goal of this practice. The goal is to learn to disagree without tension.

Confirmation bias has negative power on you as long as you can't accept that others are wired for different confirmations. When you can accept opposing views—confirmations—this bias will lose its confrontational aspect. It will become nothing more than it is, a thought which doesn't have to harm your life. Thoughts by themselves don't do any damage. Only if we react to them in a harmful manner will they deteriorate our relationships, reputation, and self-image.

Chapter 8: Empathy Gap

Empathy gap is our tendency to underestimate the power of feelings and their impact on others and ourselves. We often discount how much influence being angry, tired, sad, hungry, in pain, etc. has on our actions and preferences.

Just like you should never underestimate the power a snack and a nap has on your energy level, you should never underestimate the impact that powerful emotions can have on your ability to make decisions, or on your actions and preferences. You might find that you become a totally different person in certain situations.

A hot-cold empathy gap is a cognitive bias in which you do not accurately estimate how much power strong feelings have over your attitude, perception, preferences, and actions. As humans, our understanding is dependent upon the emotional state we are currently in. It is difficult for someone who is depressed to understand what it is like to feel happy, and vice versa. When someone is furious, it is hard for them to understand what it's like to be calm. If you are in love with someone, it is hard to remember what it felt like when you weren't or to imagine what it would be like to no longer be in love in the future.[xxii]

This empathy gap is not only limited to understanding the power our own feelings have over our lives. It also means we need to understand the power of others' feelings; how do their feelings affect them or how many others' feelings affect us.

Being unable to narrow the empathy gap can have negative consequences. For example, doctors need to be able to accurately assess how much physical pain a patient is in in order to treat them correctly, bosses need to understand when an employee might need to take some extended leave from work for bereavement, and judges need to be able to assign a fitting sentence for people who have committed a crime.

When people are in a hot state, it means they are currently impacted by strong feelings. In the hot state, they don't realize how much effect their feelings have on their actions and attitude. They misinterpret the short-term goal as being a reflection of their long-term preferences, instead of seeing it for the temporary feeling that it is.

When people are in a cold state, things are fine. They are calm and relaxed without really strong feelings driving them. When they are in a cold state, they have a hard time imagining how they would react if they were in a hot state. They forget how powerful an influence emotions can be, and as a result, are often not prepared when situations involving powerful emotions arise.

People typically struggle in these three areas of empathy gaps:

- Intrapersonal prospective: being unable to accurately predict how they would act in the future if they were in a different state than the one they are currently in.

- Intrapersonal retrospective: trying to remember and understand actions that happened in the past when they were in a different state than the one they are currently in.

- Interpersonal: trying to understand the actions and preferences of someone else who is in a different state than they are currently in.[xxiii]

How does it affect us?

There was a study conducted at Berkley College in 2001 by Dan Ariely, author of the book *Predictably Irrational*,[xxiv] and other researchers that revealed some troubling insight into the empathy gap which has implications for all of us in our daily lives. This study asked a group of male students at Berkley who were aged eighteen or older to answer a series of questions while they were in the cold state of not being sexually aroused. These questions revolved around the students predicting what their feelings and actions regarding sexual activity would be when they were in the hot state of arousal. The participants were then asked the same questions when they were aroused, and their answers were compared. The study was conducted in the hopes that it might shed some light on some major societal problems like teenage pregnancy, the transmission of sexually transmitted diseases, and HIV/AIDS, among others.

The results revealed that across the board, the participants seemed to underestimate how their actions, beliefs, and preferences would change once they were impacted by intense feelings of sexual arousal. They were confident in their answers and predictions and then found out that they did not know themselves as well as they thought once they were under the influence of very powerful feelings.

When asked about their willingness to engage in immoral behavior, their answers were quite different when they were aroused than when they were not. The percentage of participants who stated they might be willing to slip a woman a drug in order to increase the chances she might have sex with them increased by 420%, and the percentage of participants who said they would continue to try to have sex with their date after she said "no" increased by 125% when they were aroused versus when they weren't.

When it came to practicing safe sexual behavior, the study showed a decrease in the percentage of participants who would definitely wear a condom by 30% and a 29% increase in the percentage of participants who view birth control as solely the woman's responsibility when they were in a state of arousal.[xxv]

We sometimes don't understand our own emotions but even more often we fail to understand others' emotions that impact their behavior.

One study showed that our general empathy gap with other people is the strongest when they are not too similar to us. The study of Gutsell and Inzlicht tested empathy of participants presented with sad members of the same ethnic background and also sad members of a different ethnic group. The participants' brain activity was much more in tune with the sadness of the members of the same racial group than with the sadness of other racial groups. Based on this observation the study suggests that it may be harder for people to empathize with those who are different than them.[xxvi] This could be an explanation of the often so unfortunately present division and discrimination between races, sexual orientations, religions, and other belief break points. Our natural tendency of not being able to understand and empathize with those who are different from us leads to prejudice, discrimination, lack of connection, and even hostility between people of different groups. Working hard to overcome the empathy gap, therefore, is of crucial importance.

What other negative effects can the empathy gap cause?

Researchers Stephens, Neal, and Overman conducted a study following which they observed that college students were more likely "to choose a longer life than a merciful death for patients their own age and much less likely to choose the same long life for elderly patients."[xxvii] Such a lack of understanding and empathy gap can be especially challenging for young doctors. Since in most cases they are younger than their patients they need to close their empathy gap if they want to properly understand the struggles older patients go through. This lack of understanding could lead them to see less value in extending the lives of the elderly versus the life of similarly aged people. [xxviii]

The medical field is another area where the uncontrolled empathy gap can lead to severe real-life consequences and biased decision.

How to fix the empathy gap?

Just being willing to study our behavior and learn more about ourselves and how some of our tendencies differ when we are in a cold state versus a hot state will go a long way toward helping us to close our empathy gap with ourselves.

To make this self-discovery, I would suggest doing some guided meditation sessions I recommended in Chapter 1. Guided meditation helps the mind to calm down and become focused. I emphasized the guided part of the meditation practice because it is much easier to follow-through with success for those who are unfamiliar with meditation or never had a satisfying meditation practice before. Guided meditation sessions usually have a knowledgeable person speaking with a deep, relaxing voice, tapping on the mental distractions we usually have.

To close our empathy gap with people who are different from us, we need to be open-minded and strive to understand that person better. We can start by focusing on our similarities. We all experience similar emotions, for example.

Auyeung and Alden conducted a study in which participants had induced social anxiety to see if in an anxious mood were they better at identifying and rating other people's negative emotions. The study concluded that yes, they were. Since in the participants' emotional memory social anxiety was a recent event, they were more likely to identify and rate similar negative emotions in others—even in people belonging to a different age group, race, gender, or religion. Since the emotions were recently experienced by the participants, they could recall it more accurately and also, see the same emotions in other human beings. [xxix]

The takeaway of this study is that if we can find a connection point between others and ourselves, relating to them based on how we have previously felt, we may become better at being empathetic with others. We could reduce our prejudices, fears, and discriminatory inclinations towards other fellow humans.

This being said, the discovery of the study is not earth-shattering. We can safely assume that every person has already experienced some form of social anxiety, fear, shame, or other negative emotions. Why do we often fail then to empathize with others regardless of the shared emotions?

The answer to this question has to be sought in our memory. The accent of the Auyeung-Alden study was that the emotional memory in participants was recent. When time distances us from a certain negative emotion, we tend to forget the impact it had on us when it was recent. On one hand, this is a useful feature of the memory, otherwise, how could we sanely process grief, loss, and other painful emotions? On the other hand, however, it can explain why we can't instantly empathize with others who go through the same emotional experience we once went through. Our memory "archived" those emotions in order to make us feel better. [xxx]

Just think about your most recent breakup. Was it a week ago? A year ago? A decade ago? What would you say to someone who has just experienced a breakup? Chances are that if you recently went through a breakup yourself you'd be much more empathetic with the other person. If you hadn't dealt with a break up for ten years you might just shrug it off like, "you'll get over it, time heals these wounds." While you'd certainly be right, this information wouldn't console someone who is choking on the devastating feeling of loss at the moment.

Therefore nurturing memories of negative emotions is better than suppressing them. In any situation, not only for the sake of overcoming the empathy gap. By making sense of negative emotions for ourselves and using the lessons learned from them to life improvement on a daily basis can also help with our empathy gap.

Try this exercise: when you're in a highly emotional situation in the near future, and you're about to react on it, take a step back and answer this question, "is what I'm about to do or say something that I'd really want to see myself doing under calm circumstances? Is my response right and proportionate?"

Also, when you see someone having an extreme emotional outburst, instead of becoming judgmental, ask yourself, "have I ever felt so bad in my life that I felt the need of such a profound expression? Or did I have the same reaction to a different situation before? What did I need then? What calmed me down?" If you find the answer to these questions, try to help the person in need with them. Your solutions might not have the same effect on the other person as they had on you but it's worth a try.

Making a conscious effort to relate to other people help us a lot in reducing the empathy gap.

Part 3

Social Biases

Chapter 10: Social Biases

The biases we will discuss in this part occur when we try to understand why people, including ourselves, act the way they do. These biases are referred to as "attributional biases" in psychology. An attributional bias is a cognitive bias that involves the errors we make when we analyze human behavior and the reasons for it. People continually make attributions about the actions of themselves and others, but errors in perception often lead to incorrect and biased evaluations of the world around them and the people in it.

Attributional biases are present in nearly every aspect of our daily lives, so it is important that we become aware and learn more about them. For example, when someone cuts in front of us in the checkout line, we are more likely to attribute their behavior to the person being rude and inconsiderate, taking their action personally rather than consider the possibility that other circumstances may have caused their behavior. Maybe they didn't realize we were trying to get in line, or they had to rush to get to an important appointment.

There are several types of attributional biases that people tend to display when they try to figure out the causes of different behaviors. I will discuss a few but by no means all of them here:

- Fundamental attribution error: This error occurs when people try to explain the behavior of others as being due to their character, rather than situational circumstances. For example, if people see that a mother does not have warm coats on her children on a cold winter day, they are more likely to assume that it is because she is an irresponsible parent who is neglecting the needs of her children than to consider the possibility that the reason might be due to circumstances like not having enough money to buy winter coats, or that they are visiting from somewhere else and were not expecting the cold temperatures.[xxxi]

- Self-serving bias: This error occurs because people tend to take credit for their successes and assign blame to outside circumstances for their failures. For example, a student who receives a good grade on an exam might attribute the success to the fact that they studied hard. A student who receives a poor grade on an exam might attribute the failure to the test questions not being worded clearly.[xxxii]

- Hostile attribution bias: This error occurs when we incorrectly interpret a behavior that is unclear as being hostile or negative toward us, rather than being innocent. For example, if you walk into a room and two people suddenly stop talking, you might assume that they were talking about you. In reality, it is possible that their conversation had just come to an end.[xxxiii]

- The Halo Effect: the tendency for a person's positive or negative traits to influence other people's overall impression of them and their character. For example, if we find an actor to be a very good comedian, we may also assume that he is happy, kind and loving, and genuinely cheerful in real life.[xxxiv]

- Trait Ascription Bias: the tendency for people to think that their personality, attitude, and actions change more than the personality, attitude, and actions of others, which they deem to be quite predictable.[xxxv]

By now I hope you have an idea what social biases largely are. Let's take a closer look at three of the most common ones:

- authority bias,

- false consensus effect,

- and illusory superiority.

Chapter 11: Authority Bias

Authority bias is the tendency of people to give more weight to the opinion of an authority figure and allow it to have a greater influence on their decisions.

Human nature tells us to trust the opinions of authority figures as being more accurate and to be more inclined to believe their opinions—no matter the content. We are raised to believe it is our duty to listen to and obey authority figures. As children, every adult around us was an authority. It is not hard to adopt the authority bias from a young age. This tendency may continue into our adulthood as well if we don't approach this bias with more awareness.

In many ways, this sense of obligation to comply with authority figures has allowed us to create civilized societies. Following established rules, norms, and laws regarding the production and distribution of resources, trade, and our behavior toward others are just a few of the ways obeying those in authority has kept us from anarchy.

As we grew up, we realized that following the advice of true authority figures was beneficial to us because they had more knowledge and power than we did in their area of expertise. Deferring to those in authority has now evolved into a shortcut for our brains. However, following authority figures blindly can make just as much damage in society. Just think about the case of Nazi Germany.

How does it affect us?

The Milgram obedience experiment conducted in 1961 established the existence of authority bias and is an excellent example of the powerful impact it can have. The goal of the experiment was to see if people would be willing to follow orders from an authority figure, even if the orders went against their moral beliefs. The participants came from a variety of backgrounds, ages, occupations, genders, and had achieved varying levels of education. There is an empathy gap at work in the experiment, as their behavior in the hot state did not align with their predictions about their expected behavior when they were in a cold state.[xxxvi]

The participants were instructed by an authority figure to assume the role of a teacher and to present pairs of words to a student—really an actor. They were to name the first word in the pair and then ask the student to name the second word. Whenever the student answered incorrectly or did not answer, the authority figure told the teacher to administer a powerful electric shock to the student. The shock was to increase in strength with every incorrect answer or answer not given. While in reality, the teacher really was not administering any more shocks except the initial small electric shock, the participants were unaware of this and truly thought they were causing the students great pain. They were told that they could stop the experiment at any time, but despite feeling guilty and stressed about hurting another person, only 34% of the participants attempted to defy the authority figure to stop inflicting what they thought were painful electric shocks on the person acting as a student. It showed a really troubling view of just how dangerous the authority bias can be.

The authority bias shows itself in how advertisers try to influence our buying decisions. In order to sell us toothpaste, dental floss, mouthwash, or even chewing gum, companies may claim that four out of five dentists recommend their product and show us actors dressed like dentists in the commercial. Even though most people realize that the people in the commercial are not actually dentists, but rather paid actors, it does not seem to impact the effectiveness of the commercial or make people question whether the claim is true. Just the mere suggestion of an endorsement of a product from an authority figure seems to be enough.

Sometimes the authority bias can fool even authority figures themselves. Few would argue that Albert Einstein was the ultimate authority figure as the prominent expert of his day—and beyond—in the field of physics. He argued strongly against Niels Bohr's theory of the atom, known as Bohr's model, claiming that it was simply impossible for him to imagine it. Einstein's arguments were proven to be incorrect, and Bohr's Model is still used today.[xxxvii]

Even the greatest thinkers in history are not immune to the authority bias. Sometimes those who are experts in their fields let their ego win out and begin to believe a little too much in their own infallibility. Everyone makes mistakes—even experts—so to blindly accept everything coming from an authority figure as the absolute truth, even if other facts contradict them, or if what they say goes against what you consider to be moral and ethical behavior, is to do yourself a real disservice.

How to fix authority bias?

We all give a special meaning to the advice of our parents, friends, idols, and experts in different fields. Yet, we need to beware of turning a blind eye and ear to those views of these authority figures that are outside of their field of expertise.

You may listen to your friend when she says, "Never buy that shampoo. It made my hair fall out like crazy." You may be inclined to listen to her because she is your friend and her remark may sound like a well-founded, empirically tested opinion. However, she is not a cosmetician, nor a doctor. Her hair loss may be due to totally different circumstances than the hair care product in question. Do your own research regarding the shampoo.

I would definitely trust my dentist with my teeth because he has taken care of them well for decades, but just because he is a good dentist doesn't mean he knows which mobile phone is the best for excessive gaming—or taking the best photographs.

We have to be careful to take personal opinion of people with a grain of salt. Question what you read and hear. Don't be afraid to ask direct questions of authority figures. This does not mean you are trying to be rude or disrespectful; it means you are trying to be informed. Just like you are encouraged to seek a second opinion when you receive a diagnosis from a doctor, seek a second opinion with the information you read and hear.

Do some research on your own. Check multiple reputable sources to see if they support or refute the information you have already encountered. If truth and accuracy are things you value, then you will appreciate the opportunity to put this thinking error to rest with just the right amount of healthy skepticism.

Chapter 12: False Consensus Effect

The false consensus effect is the tendency for people to overestimate how much others agree with them. Studies showed that there are three main reasons why false consensus occurs:

1. Similar attracts similar and we are a mish-mash of the five people we spend our most time with. These people are most likely our close friends and family. People so close to each other are likely to be similar and share many of the same beliefs and behaviors.

2. Humans are creatures who seek pleasure and avoid pain. Feeling that someone is not agreeing with us can be disturbing or

painful, thus we prefer ditching this notion when we have no empirical evidence. What do we do instead? We believe that other people think and act the same way we do. Why? Because thinking like this makes us feel good about ourselves.

3. Because of availability heuristic. We are the most aware of our own thoughts and values and when we are trying to estimate how common our values are, we are likely to search for examples that come to our minds the quickest. Since these ideas are in our awareness and dictate our, we are more likely to notice when other people share similar ideas and values.

What is the false consensus effect?

The false consensus effect is an attributional cognitive bias in which we tend to think our opinions, beliefs, values, preferences, and habits are a reflection of those who are normal and rational human beings. This leads us to perceive that others think like us, and to believe in a consensus that does not exist, called a "false consensus." A false consensus makes us feel good. It increases our self-esteem and confidence and makes us feel like we fit in and belong.[xxxviii]

Social media plays to our sense of false consensus as we often see things in our news feed that support certain political positions. Because this comes, in part, from the people we follow and an algorithm that makes calculations about our preferences, it may cause us to incorrectly estimate the number of people who agree with our opinions.

The false consensus effect was first named in the late 1970s by Lee Ross and a group of his colleagues, who conducted a series of research experiments asking the participants to read a scenario in which there was a conflict.[xxxix] The participants were then presented with two possible ways of responding to the conflict. They were asked to choose which way they thought the conflict should be resolved, and then to guess which option they thought other people would choose. Further, they were asked to describe what type of people they thought would select each option of resolving the conflict.

The study found that regardless of which choice the participants picked, they also tended to think that the majority of other people would make the same choice. The participants also tended to assign the more negative descriptions to the people who they identified as likely to choose the option they did not.

How does the false consensus effect affect us?

The false consensus effect is connected to the availability heuristic in that when we try to guess how likely something is to occur, we tend to look at the examples that pop into our minds right away.

When we assess whether our beliefs are shared by others, it is likely that the first people who come to our mind are those who we think of as being similar to us, like our family, friends, and colleagues, because we think we have a lot in common with them.

There are times when the false consensus effect seems to be strongest, causing us to believe that more people agree with us: when we feel really passionately about something, when we are really confident that our beliefs and opinions are correct, and when we think that others are in the same boat experiencing things exactly as we are.

Why is it hard to research?

We don't know what personal traits make people more likely to develop a false consensus effect. It is entirely possible for people within the same social group to have two very different levels of this cognitive bias, but we have not yet identified what personal or social differences may contribute to their different responses.

It can be difficult to gather accurate data about the false consensus effect because experiments often require participants to commit to being involved for an extended period of time. Due to most people having responsibilities that would prevent them from being able to do this, groups studied often consist of participants like college students who can make such a commitment. College students do not accurately represent an adequate sample of society as a whole, which can cause experiment results to be skewed.

How to fix it?

As with most of the other biases we have already discussed in the book, the first step to overcoming the false consensus effect is acknowledging its existence and effect on us. Take some time to learn about it, and then commit to doing something to overcome it. If the false consensus effect is impacting you in business, expand the group from whom you seek feedback and opinions. Don't just rely on input from your colleagues or those who you know will agree with you. When you ask for advice from someone who would support your views no matter what, you're truly seeking comfort and confirmation, not advice. Expand your source of information, conduct tests, and surveys, and don't just assume you know what others think.

Do this exercise now: try to come up with three beliefs you hold that you are convinced the majority of people would agree with? When you are done, spend ten minutes on the internet for each belief and try to find confirmation bias-free data to verify if you are right or not.

You can apply the same principles to your personal life. Expand your horizons beyond the news channels you typically watch or the information that pops up on your social media accounts. Realize that there is a great big world out there filled with people who do not share the same opinions as you. Accept people of different faiths and cultures and respect their rights to have their own cherished beliefs, which may be quite different than your own.

Recognize that we are all just people trying to navigate life's journey, and there are many different paths to get where we're going. It's perfectly fine to agree to disagree. We don't all need to fit the same mold. That's what makes life more interesting, and there's absolutely nothing wrong with that.

Chapter 13: Illusory Superiority

Illusory superiority is the tendency to overestimate our positive traits and underestimate our negative ones as we compare ourselves to others.

The term "illusory superiority" was first used in 1991 by researchers Van Yperen and Buunk. It is a positive—albeit often incorrect—image we hold of ourselves as we seek to compare ourselves to others. When affected by the illusory superiority bias, people tend to overestimate their level of intelligence, performance on tasks, and positive personal character and personality traits as they compare to others.[xl]

If you think in terms of comparing the performance of people statistically, fifty percent of people should fall below average and fifty percent of people should fall above average. However, in a study conducted about driving skills, about two third of Americans identify themselves as being above average, or even excellent drivers. This is simply mathematically impossible.[xli]

But do they have such a positive attitude about every driver on the road? Not really.

Research showed that the drivers' positive rating of others is more than twice as low as their self-rating. For example, only twenty-nine percent of the surveyed people gave above average or excellent rating to their closest friends, and even less, twenty-two percent gave these labels to drivers of their own age.

In other words, A thinks he's an excellent driver and B is below average to bad, while B thinks she's a terrific driver and A is terrible. They can't both be right.

The AAA Foundation for Traffic Safety conducted a survey of traffic culture attitudes. They wanted to track some repeating trends they had observed in prior years.[xlii]

In the previous years, their survey concluded that some aspects of our traffic safety culture are a culture of indifference. Drivers often have a "Do as I say, not as I do" mindset. For example, many drivers, when asked, state that it is unacceptable and reckless to drive 15 mph over the speed limit on freeways. However, they also admitted to speeding in the not so distant past. Of course, they perceive that for them, as being excellent drivers, it is okay to speed from time to time. They are not the problem, but all those other incompetent drivers who speed…

This phenomenon shows what illusory superiority is quite accurately.

How does it affect us?

The Dunning-Kruger effect

In 1999, social psychologists David Dunning and Justin Kruger conducted a study where the participants were given a specific job: solve logic problems, analyze grammar questions, or decide whether jokes were funny or not. They were asked to judge their level of performance on their task by comparing themselves to the other participants.

Dunning and Kruger divided the participants into four groups according to their performance. All of the groups judged their own performance to be above average. The group who received the lowest performance scores from others had the greatest illusory superiority bias. The researchers concluded that people who are the worst at performing satisfactorily on tasks are also poor at identifying the skills necessary to perform the tasks well. Once the lowest scoring group received training in the task, their performance level improved, and so did their ability to more accurately assess their own skills.

People of lower ability make the mistake of thinking their ability is greater than it really is. This is because they are lacking the self-awareness that would allow them to recognize their own weaknesses. This thinking error makes it impossible for them to accurately judge their own level of competence when it comes to a given trait, skill, or task. This mistake often results in failure which leads to other negative consequences like decreased self-esteem, anger, a state of internal conflict.

Errors in self-assessment also occur in the people who are actually the best performers on a given task. They often mistakenly underestimate their ability level, because they assume that since the task is easy for them, it is probably easy for others as well.

There seems to be a difference in the Dunning-Kruger effect between cultures. While Dunning and Kruger focused their study in North America, where self-esteem is highly valued, and found that Americans tend to overestimate their abilities and traits in comparison with others, other studies have found that in cultures where the value is placed on self-improvement in order to make yourself more helpful to the group, like in Japan, the tendency is for people to underestimate their abilities and traits, thinking that there is always room for improvement.[xliii]

Illusory superiority is not only limited to areas of mental ability like intelligence, memory, and performance on tasks. It extends to other areas as well. It occurs when we compare ourselves to others in terms of how popular we perceive ourselves to be, or how happy we think we are in our relationships. Illusory superiority affects the way we see ourselves when it comes to our behavior, wellbeing, driving skills, sense of humor, and even the ability to avoid bias.

When we hold ourselves in such high regard, often without anything to back up our opinions, it prevents us from being able to recognize our weaknesses and work to improve them.

How to fix it?

The problem illusory superiority presents us with is that when our skills and traits are lacking, we are unable to recognize it and understand what we need to do in order to improve them. This can create a cycle that is hard to break. Often illusory superiority seem harmless—I bet you could name at least three pompous fools in your acquaintance circle that you have accustomed yourself with and accepted their ridiculous overestimation of their strengths. I'm also sure that you don't want to be one of these fools. Illusory superiority makes people—seem—ignorant, having a negative

143

correlation with development and maturity, and has a greater effect on how others label and treat these people.

If you identified yourself as someone who often falls into this bias, there are some practices you can do to minimize its influence on you.

One way of avoiding illusory superiority is willfully becoming open and tolerant of the views and perspectives of other people. You have a particular way of looking at things, but so do others. Also, consider the option that your self-assessment might not always be right. If you keep your mind open and diminish your snap judgments—whether they are positive or negative—and restrain yourself from thoughts such as being the epitome of intelligence, you will know that there is always room for improvement. In anything. For everyone.

This brings us to the next step—never stop learning. One of the key differences between people with and without illusory superiority is that the latter are committed to never stop learning. People like Bill Gates or the Dalai Lama read every day for the sole purpose of learning and improving. How could they reach their success level otherwise?

It is difficult sometimes to make an accurate self-judgment on how good we really are in something. To avoid falling prey to illusory superiority, get an unbiased view on yourself by someone who can give you a fluff-free opinion. Family and friends might not be the best choice as they either naturally see you through their loving-biased lens, or they don't want to hurt your feelings. Stay open to constructive criticism. Overcoming illusory superiority is often a painful road including the acceptance that you may not be as good as you think you are. But that doesn't make you a less valuable or good person.

Being objective and more realistic about who you are is, in fact, a powerful knowledge. It shows you where you need to improve more, saves you from engaging in battles you couldn't possibly win, and shelters you from making a fool of yourself. Eventually, with hard work, and purposeful learning you can actually become the great singer, smart debater, engaging public speaker you wish to be.

Chapter 14: Ingroup Bias

Ingroup bias is the tendency for people to treat others better if they think they belong to their own groups. Marilynn Brewer said, "Ultimately, many forms of discrimination and bias may develop not because outgroups are hated, but because positive emotions such as admiration, sympathy, and trust are reserved for the ingroup."

Most of the time, ingroup bias doesn't occur because people dislike another group, but rather it comes from showing preference to their own group. Many times when showing favoritism through ingroup bias leads to discrimination toward outgroups. When we give our own group better treatment, it can come at the expense of others.

An ingroup is a social group that a person identifies with and feels a connection to. An outgroup is a group that a person doesn't feel connected to or able to identify with. Sometimes the favoritism that we show toward our own group stems from us feeling the need to compete with other groups because there are a limited amount of resources available to us, or because we want to prove that our group is superior to others.[xliv]

It is one thing to have positive feelings for and treat our group with kindness and compassion, but it is another thing entirely when we think we should, in turn, feel negative about other groups and treat them poorly. This, just like the empathy gap, can create one of the ugliest problems facing our society today: discrimination and inequality.

Why do so many people fall into this thinking error so easily? Because the ingroup bias evolutionarily serves an important purpose; it creates stability and harmony in the group and makes it more likely that the group will continue to thrive. Like so many other cognitive biases, ingroup bias can be taken too far, and if taken to an extreme, it can create harmful consequences.

How does it affect us?

Let's take a simple, yet representative example. Sports fans are extremely loyal to their teams and sometimes have intense negative feelings toward opposing teams, and even that team's fans. It is not unusual to hear cruel comments being shouted at the players and fans of rival teams. Many sports venues try to sell tickets in such a way as to seat the fans of opposing teams separate from one another in order to keep things from getting out of hand as emotions run high.

A study on ingroup bias

A well-known study called Sherif's Robbers' Cave Experiment demonstrated how competing for resources can lead to ingroup bias. A mock summer camp was set up, and twenty-two boys from similar backgrounds were split into two groups for the purpose of the study. In the beginning, the boys thought that everyone belongs to the same group, the camp. They were even encouraged to bond. In the next part of the experiment, the research conductors separated the boys into two groups and made them compete against each other for resources. The researchers observed that after the split, the boys greatly favored the people in their own group but were often openly mean to members of the opposing group. Even if they knew these people from earlier and were on good terms with them.[xlv]

How to fix it?

Ingroup bias can have significant negative consequences and quickly escalates to form horrible and lasting prejudices. Children may be bullied and be excluded from groups, causing them to feel depressed and alone. In the workplace, cliques can affect the way that people work together, and ultimately the productivity and efficiency of the business can suffer.

In the absolute worst-case scenario, ingroup bias can lead to life-threatening consequences between groups who view each other as enemies and engage in war.

As a parent or a person in power, you can try to break ingroup bias in children or young adults by shielding the identity of groups from each other. There are no groups. Everyone is human. That's the "group." Do this with race, gender, religious, and other crucial social break lines. This is especially important at the thought generation stage where ingroup bias can influence the ideas generated. If someone grows up without the black-white group, gay-straight group, Christian—Muslim—Atheist—Hindu—etc.—distinctions, they are less likely to discriminate other people based on these characteristics.

As an adult, already conditioned to fall into this bias, you need to recognize that it is very difficult to overcome. Even if you try, it's unlikely you will be able to eliminate it completely. The best thing you can do is to continue to question yourself "am I acting because of the influence of ingroup bias?"

Acknowledge that the pressure to conform can easily mislead people. Biases are nothing more and nothing less than a systematic disparity between our beliefs—the things we accept as true—and objective reality—what is actually true.

Our brain makes us susceptible to bias, and to minimize or overcome the impact of bias requires a great deal of presence, self-reflective ability, and open-mindedness.

To avoid being biased, you need to be ready to recognize and admit when you are wrong. Biased people hardly ever admit if they are wrong. They may recognize it sometimes but even then they are not likely to admit it. This is likely due to their ego and hubris rather than actually being objectively correct all the time.

Be open-minded, humble, ready to be wrong, and be prepared to change your mind when needed.

Part 4

Memory errors and biases

Chapter 15: Memory Errors and Biases

A memory bias is a cognitive bias that either helps or hinders the recall of a memory. This could involve the likelihood of a memory being able to be remembered, or how long it takes for the memory to be accessed, or some combination of the two. Some biases even change the content of the memory.

There are many types of memory biases. Some of them are:

- Context effect—Memory relies on context. If memories are out of context, they will be harder to recall than those that are in context. This is why sometimes we need to retrace our steps and start over again in order to remember something. Being in your office at work may make it easier to recall important details from a meeting or phone call, or returning to your alma mater for a class reunion may make it easier to remember events you experienced in high school or college. [xlvi]

- Cross race effect—The tendency for people belonging to one race to have trouble identifying people of another race. This can be seen when a witness tries to recognize someone belonging to a race other than their own. Sometimes they may feel that all of the faces appear too similar to them, and they are not able to distinguish between them. In this case, they are able to be more detailed in the descriptions of members of their own race.[xlvii]

- Peak-end rule—People tend to not think of a complete experience when they are determining if it was enjoyable or not. Instead, they focus on the average of how it felt at its peak and how it ended. It seems that we are all looking for a happy ending and like to go out on a high note. When that happens, we rate the experience as being more pleasant overall.[xlviii]

- Processing difficulty effect—Information that we have to spend more time reading and thinking about in order to understand is easier for us to remember.[xlix]

- Spotlight effect—This is the tendency for people to overestimate how much others will notice or pay attention to your appearance and behavior. If you have ever been horrified to arrive at work only to notice that you are wearing two different colored shoes, or ever had to deal with a crying child in the store and were so embarrassed because you felt like everyone was staring at you, then you have experienced the spotlight effect firsthand.[1]

- Tip of the tongue phenomenon—When a person can remember parts of an object or some information but cannot remember the whole item. Experts think this may be "blocking" at work, where similar memories are being remembered at the same time and start to interfere with one another, preventing the full memory from being accessible. This happens when you can picture someone or something in your head, but you can't remember the person's name or the word you are trying to say. You might remember the letter it starts with, or part of the word, and feel like it's going to pop into your head at any moment. It's frustrating until it does.[li]

Knowing some of the memory biases you may experience can be quite helpful. At the very least, you will know they are natural occurrences, and you are certainly not alone in experiencing them. Let's take a closer look at some of the most common memory biases, egocentric bias, and the illusion of truth effect.

Chapter 16: Egocentric Bias

Egocentric bias is when people remember the past in a way that strokes their ego. They only pay attention to their own point of view, and they often think more highly of themselves than the facts would support. For example, they may remember winning a race by a greater margin or a faster time or remember earning better grades and a bigger scholarship than what really occurred.

You know the type of person I'm talking about— the guy who tells you he caught a twenty-inch fish right after you share that the fish you caught was twelve inches long. Or the old friend who says she had four guys trying to ask her to prom when your memory of that event in high school is that it was only one—the one she asked out. They are often the life of the party with many colorful stories to tell, but they don't realize that people take what they say with a grain of salt because they feel like their boastful tales are not accurate. They are the ones who always want to feel superior to others, and their egocentric bias memories help them to achieve those results, if only in their own minds.

What is egocentric bias?

An egocentric bias occurs when people spend too much time thinking about things from only their own perspective, and their thinking becomes distorted as they start to believe their own hype. This bias makes people start to see themselves as more important and influential than reality would suggest. They may think that they alone were responsible for winning the big game, or for closing the big deal at work. In their mind, they contributed to the successful outcomes far more than they really did.[lii]

People with egocentric biases will think that they are above average and superior to their peers in nearly every area imaginable. They may also come to feel invincible, like bad things such as an accident or a poor medical diagnosis are unlikely to happen to them.

This bias was first named in 1980 by a psychologist from Ohio State University named Anthony Greenwald. He believes that egocentric biases are when a person's beliefs become so skewed that what they recall from their memory is different than what really happened.

Egocentric bias happens when people stop looking at things from the perspective of others. When people only focus on how much they personally have done, it is very easy for them to feel like their contributions to a group effort are far greater than they really are. Daniel Schacter, a Harvard

University psychology professor, refers to egocentric bias as one of the "seven sins" of memory.[liii]

People who are greatly impacted by egocentric bias often choose friends and social groups based on how much positive feedback they receive from their exaggerated stories, as it serves to continue to stroke their ego.

How does egocentric bias affect us?

There was a study conducted in 1993 in Japan where researchers asked participants to write about fair or unfair events that they or others were privy to. The study found that people tend to start writing about fair events using the word "I" and unfair events using the word "others." This showed that they felt responsible for successes while assigning the blame for failures to other people. The study did note a difference between Japanese women and men. Women were more likely than men to remember the actions of others more than their own and also seemed to assign fair and unfair behaviors more to others than themselves.[liv]

A study conducted by Greenberg found the egocentric bias impacts what people view as being fair or unfair. Participants identified overpayment to themselves as being fairer than others getting overpaid. Additionally, they thought it was more unfair when they themselves were underpaid than when others were. This egocentric bias was only lessened when Greenberg made the participants more self-aware by having them look in a mirror as they responded. He found that this made them have one set standard of what was fair for both themselves and others. It was then that the participants felt both overpayment and underpayment were unfair, no matter who was receiving the money. He believed self-awareness to be key in limiting egocentric bias.[lv]

A study conducted by Paula Rubio-Fernandez and Sam Glucksberg found that bilingual people are less likely to be impacted by egocentric bias than people who only speak one language. They concluded that because people who are bilingual spend a lot of time listening to the thoughts of others, they are less likely to only focus on and remember their own point of view.[lvi]

Egocentric bias means that people tend to view their own contributions to a group effort or relationship as being more valuable than those of the other people involved. When you ask married couples who are more responsible for positive activities—like taking out the trash—or negative activities—like starting arguments—both spouses are likely to identify themselves as the responsible party in either case. When siblings have been asked which of them contributes more to the family, the majority of them thought that they themselves contributed more than their siblings.

However, siblings who were observed or reported to have a closer relationship with one another showed less egocentric bias and more objective accuracy when identifying the contributions that they and their siblings made to the family.

Egocentric bias may impact a person's decision about whether or not to vote in an election. People who display some egocentric bias are likely to believe that their vote counts and may overestimate the significance of their one individual ballot. They also are likely to consider the false consensus effect when casting their vote and want to contribute to a victory for those who share similar values and opinions. A study of the 2008 American presidential election found that when voters strongly favor one candidate over the other, they are more likely to be convinced that the candidate they support will win. Those who strongly favored Barack Obama in the election believed he had a 65% chance of becoming president on average, while those who supported his opponent predicted that Obama only had a 40% chance of winning.[lvii]

Having a very high or very low egocentric bias may be a sign of a possible mental illness. There is a healthy and happy medium. People who display a great deal of egocentric bias may suffer from an anxiety disorder, as they tend to view themselves as being the center of attention in all things. Depression may be present in those with very low levels of egocentric bias. Studies have shown that people who are depressed are far more accurate in assessing their contributions to groups than those who are not, which would seem to indicate that they are much less egocentric.

What to do about egocentric bias?

It's extremely difficult for any human being to escape egocentrism. We experience situations, create perceptions, and fuel expectations based on our own worldview. We experience our entire life from our heads. Thus it's not surprising that we become biased in our own favor.

Since spending too much time only seeing the world from our own perspective seems to be the catalyst for egocentric bias to kick in, the first step of overcoming it is getting out of our own heads. If we can just step back and see things from another point of view, it goes a long way in taking the focus off ourselves, and in turn, reducing our egocentrism.

Engage in egocentrism-correction actions following these five steps recommended by Susan Kraus Whitbourne Ph.D., who is a Professor Emerita of Psychological and Brain Sciences at the University of Massachusetts Amhers.

"1. Make an honest assessment of your egocentric behaviors. Take stock of the behaviors caused by ordinary egocentrism that may be getting out of control (...) and decide whether you're letting your internal viewpoint skew your social interactions.

2. Check out how other people feel (…) by putting yourself in their place. Using active empathic listening, for example, you can broaden your perspective to see not just from the inside out, but from the outside in.

3. Build up your inner sense of self. Don't let your self-definition become too dependent on receiving attention from others. Find ways to build your self-esteem by developing an internal set of standards that allow you to reward yourself for your actual accomplishments.

4. Squelch your imaginary audience. You may feel that everyone is looking at you and judging you, but in reality, most people are just as concerned about themselves as they are about you.

5. Practice counter-egocentrism. Test out your abilities to take another person's point of view by trying to explain that skill of yours to someone

who's never attempted the task in question. Read over your e-mails before you send them to make sure you haven't skipped over details that only you know about."[lviii]

Chapter 17: Illusion of Truth Effect

The illusion of truth effect is the tendency for people to believe things that they have heard before, even if they do not remember actually consciously hearing them, and even if the statement hasn't been proven to be valid. It's the familiarity that seems to be a source of comfort, and it creates a sense of believing something to be true. The illusion of truth effect was first defined in 1977 following a study conducted by Villanova University and Temple University. This study asked the college student participants to identify a group of statements as being true or false. [lix]

The researchers, Lynn Hasher, David Goldstein, and Thomas Toppino, gave the participants lists of sixty believable sentences, some of which were true and some of which were false. The lists were given to the participants in two-week intervals. Twenty of the statements were repeated on each list, while the other forty were unique to each individual list. The statements were designed to be about things the students were not likely to know the answers to, and they were asked to rank their confidence about whether each statement was true or false on a scale from one to seven. With the forty new statements, the participants' confidence did not change from one list to the other. With the twenty repeated statements, their confidence increased with each exposure to them. The researchers concluded that the repetition of information makes it more likely to be accepted as fact.[lx] In 1989, Hal R. Arkes, Catherine Hackett, and Larry Boehm repeated the initial study and observed similar results.[lxi]

In a study conducted in 2015, researchers Lisa K. Fazio, Nadia M. Brasier, B. Keith Payne, and Elizabeth J. Marsh found that familiarity can actually prove powerful enough to overrule legitimate known facts. The illusion of truth effect was at work when the participants in the study knew information was correct but were convinced to doubt it when incorrect information disputing it was repeated over and over. When people hear information multiple times, their brains respond to it more quickly and interpret that as a signal that the information is true. It seems simply repeating false information is enough to sway the opinions of many people.[lxii]

When people try to decide if information is true, they try to measure it against what they already know is true and familiar to them. The repetition of information makes it easier to digest and understand, and ultimately, easier to remember.

Processing fluency

Initially, it was believed that the illusion of the truth effect would only happen if people were absolutely unsure about information they were presented with. Psychologists believed that things that seemed unbelievable would not demonstrate the same results with this effect. It turns out they were wrong. An example that proved they were wrong can be taken from a 2015 study. Most people know that Scottish people wear short skirts called kilts. However, the participants in the study were repeatedly presented with the statement, "A sari is the name of the short, plaid skirt worn by the Scots." Even though the participants knew the correct information prior to the study taking place, multiple exposures to the incorrect statement were enough to make many of them identify it as being true.[lxiii]

The researchers call this processing fluency. When information is repeated, it becomes easier for people to understand as opposed to new information that they are unfamiliar with. People perceive information that they can easily understand to be true.

Hindsight Bias

Ralph Hertwig, Gerd Gigerenzer, and Ulrich Hoffrage conducted a study in 1997 which connected the illusion of the truth effect with "hindsight bias."[lxiv] Hindsight bias is when people claim that they knew and predicted an outcome all along after an event has already happened. They can make the same claims when it comes to whether information is true or false after it has already been confirmed or disputed.

The illusion of the truth effect has only been studied recently, but it is something people have been aware of for thousands of years. Leaders all throughout history have found a way of utilizing the repetition necessary to their advantage. They often used repeated phrases and affirmations to help unite their followers behind their goals. Among them are Cato, Napoleon, Quintillian, Ronald Reagan, and many more.

How does it affect us?

If a lie is repeated often enough, it will be seen as the truth. The more people are willing to share information that they do not know for certain is true, the more difficult it becomes for everyone to be able to distinguish between truths and lies.

Repetition carries with it the power of persuasion. It is used by everyone, from politicians to advertising executives, to parents trying to get kids to clean their rooms and do their homework. Some studies have shown that repeating information between three and five times produces the best results of inspiring people's confidence in believing it as established fact. Sometimes the repetition doesn't even need to enter our conscious thoughts. Advertisers bank on the ability of their sales pitch to seep into our minds through catchy slogans and jingles when we aren't really paying attention.

When we work in groups, if one person is able to communicate their view more than once, the other group members tend to assign more weight to it than the opinions of other group members.

How to handle the illusory truth effect?

Now that we are aware of the illusion of the truth effect, we can begin to protect ourselves from falling prey to it. We need to be willing to double-check information before we accept it as true. Try to find the information in multiple reliable sources so you can prove its validity.

Don't take for granted that something is true just because you have heard it more than once. Stop repeating things you have heard unless you have done the work to prove that they are true. Facts should matter. It seems that we are forgetting that a little too often these days.

In order to make an informed and rational decision, we need to diligently search various types of sources and fact-check statements to make an informed decision or form an accurate opinion. This obviously was a difficult and tedious task to do. However, without doing it the best chance we'll get to gain accurate knowledge is fifty percent. It's either true or not. While fifty percent might not sound a devastatingly scary ratio, think about it this way, if your doctor said the surgery you're about to undergo has a fifty percent chance of survival rate, would you still do it?—Let's not consider cases where the alternative of such a surgery is 100% death.

Investigate before you repeat information so that you don't inadvertently spread a lie and contribute to a world where the line between fact and fiction becomes more blurred by the day.

Final Thoughts

In order to keep everything on track and expend the least amount of mental energy possible so that it can be saved for other things, our brains have come to rely on some shortcuts to help them do their jobs. There are times these shortcuts can lead us astray and cause us to make some critical thinking errors. The first step to overcoming these thinking errors is to become aware of their existence. If left unchecked, these errors may come to stand between us and the truth, preventing us from making informed, positive decisions for our lives.

We can avoid becoming the victim of our biases by continually evaluating our cognitive patterns, plan out alternative reactions to biases, and revising our evaluation as necessary.

While we can't rid ourselves from biased thinking for good, it's not impossible to diminish their effect on our lives. Being honest with ourselves about our biases; admitting that we don't know everything about our thinking patterns, and that is okay; challenging our assumptions and encouraging others to do the same; seeking valuable feedback from a third-party to make sure we're heading to the right direction can all help us become better people.

If you feel that your biases are poisoning your life and you can't work on them alone, seek out professional help on how to deal with them.

Remember, no matter how fair-minded and well-intentioned you are, the inescapable reality is that we all have inherent biases. You are not bad, crazy, or more irrational than others. You're just a human being like the rest of us. Embrace it.

Increase your awareness and strive to become
your best self every day.
185

Steven

Reference

Alley Dog. *Actor-Observer Bias*. Alley Dog. 2018.
https://www.alleydog.com/glossary/definition.php?term=Actor-Observer%20Bias

Anderson, K. B., Anderson, C. A., Dill, K. E., Deuser, W. E. *The interactive relations between trait hostility, pain and aggressive thoughts.* Aggressive Behavior, 24, 161-171. 1988.

Ariely, Dan. *Predictably Irrational.* Harper Collins. 2009.

Bloom, C., Bloom, L. *The Bandwagoon Effect.* Psychology Today. 2017.

https://www.psychologytoday.com/blog/stronger-the-broken-places/201708/the-bandwagon-effect

Boyd, Andrew. *No. 2627 - Einstein – Bohr Debates*. The University of Houston. 2010. https://www.uh.edu/engines/epi2627.htm

Boyes, Alice. PhD. *The Self-Serving Bias - Definition, Research, and Antidotes*. Psychology Today. 2013. https://www.psychologytoday.com/blog/in-practice/201301/the-self-serving-bias-definition-research-and-antidotes

Cassad, Bettina J. *Confirmation Bias*. Britannica. 2018. https://www.britannica.com/topic/confirmation-bias

Changing Minds. *Context Effect*. Changing Minds. 2016.

http://changingminds.org/explanations/preferences/context_effect.htm

Changing Minds. *Fundamental Attribution Error.* Changing Minds. 2018. http://changingminds.org/explanations/theories/fundamental_attribution_error.htm

Chen, Ting., Sun, Xiaomin. *Shared information bias in group decision-making: Based on hidden profile paradigm.* Advances in Psychological Science, 24(1): 132-142. 2016.

Collins, Allan, M. Loftus Elizabeth F. *A Spreading Activation Theory of Semantic Processing. Psychological Review. 82. 407-428. 10.1037//0033-295X.82.6.407. 1975.*

Elder, L. Paul, R. Becoming a Critic Of Your Thinking. The Foundation for Critical Thinking. 2017.

http://www.criticalthinking.org/pages/becoming-a-critic-of-your-thinking/478

Fazio, Lisa K., Brashier, Nadia M., Payne, B. Keith., Marsh, Elizabeth J. *Knowledge does not protect against illusory truth (PDF)*. Journal of Experimental Psychology: General. 144 (5): 993–1002.   2015. https://web.archive.org/web/20160514233138/https://www.apa.org/pubs/journals/features/xge-0000098.pdf

Gilovich, T., Medvec, V. H., Savitsky, K. (2000). *The spotlight effect in social judgment: An egocentric bias in estimates of the salience of one's own actions and appearance.* Journal of Personality and Social Psychology, 78 (02), 211–222. 2000.

Greenberg, Jerald. *Overcoming Egocentric Bias in Perceived Fairness Through Self-Awareness.*

Social Psychology Quarterly 46, no. 2, 152-56. 1983. http://www.jstor.org/stable/3033852

Hasher, L., Goldstein, D., Toppino, T. *Frequency and the conference of referential validity*. Journal of Verbal Learning & Verbal Behaviour 16(1): 107–112. 1977.

Hertwig, Ralph. Gigerenzer, Gerd. Hoffrage, Ulrich. The Reiteration Effect in Hindsight Bias. Center for Adaptive Behavior and Cognition. 2001. https://www.mpib-berlin.mpg.de/volltexte/institut/dok/full/hertwig/hr reipr_/hrreipr_.html

Hoorens, Vera. *Self-enhancement and Superiority Biases in Social Comparison*. European Review of Social Psychology. Psychology Press. 4 (1): 113–139. 1993.

Jenkins, Aric. Which Is Safer: Airplanes or Cars? Fortune. 2017. http://fortune.com/2017/07/20/are-airplanes-safer-than-cars/

Kahneman, Daniel. *Thinking Fast And Slow.* Farrar, Straus and Giroux. 2013.

Kahneman, D., Tversky, A. *Evaluation by moments: Past and future.* In D. Kahneman & A. Tversky (Eds.), Choices, values and frames (pp. 2-23). New York: Cambridge University Press. 1999.

Kammer, D. *Differences in trait ascriptions to self and friend: Unconscious founding intensity from variability.* Psychological Reports 51, 99-102. 1982. http://psychology.wikia.com/wiki/Trait_ascription_bias

Kendra, Cherry. *What is the Ingroup Bias? Explore Psychology. 2016.* *https://www.explorepsychology.com/ingroup-bias/*

Lerner, Jennifer., Tetlock, Philip. *Accounting for the Effects of Accountability.* American Psychology Association, Psychological Bulletin Vol. 125., No. 2. 225-275. 1999. https://scholar.harvard.edu/files/jenniferlerner/files/lerner_and_tetlock_1999_pb_paper.pdf

Loewenstein, G. *Hot-cold empathy gaps and medical decision-making.* Health Psychology, 24(Suppl. 4), S49-S56. 2005.

McLeod, Saul. *The Milgram Experiment.* Simply Psychology. 2007. https://www.simplypsychology.org/milgram.html

Murphy, Mark. *The Dunning-Kruger Effect Shows Why Some People Think They're Great Even When*

Their Work Is Terrible. Forbes. 2017. https://www.forbes.com/sites/markmurphy/2017/01/24/the-dunning-kruger-effect-shows-why-some-people-think-theyre-great-even-when-their-work-is-terrible/#619edf465d7c

Murray, Bridget. The seven sins of memory American Psychological Association. 2003.http://www.apa.org/monitor/oct03/sins.aspx

O'Brien, Edward J., Myers, Jerome L. *When comprehension difficulty improves memory for text*. Journal of Experimental Psychology: Learning, Memory, and Cognition. 11 (1): 12–21. 1985.

Ofir, C., Raghubir, P., Brosh, G., Monroe, K. B., Heiman, A. *Memory-based store price judgments: the role of knowledge and shopping experience.* Journal of Retailing, 84(4), 414-423. 2008.

Peer, Eyal., Gamliel, Eyal. *Heuristics and Biases in Judicial Decisions.* NCSC. 2018. http://aja.ncsc.dni.us/publications/courtrv/cr49-2/CR49-2Peer.pdf

Pollage, Danielle C. *Making up History: False Memories of Fake News Stories.* Europe's Journal of Psychology. Vol. 8(2), 245–250. 2012. https://ejop.psychopen.eu/index.php/ejop/article/viewFile/456/pdf

Psychology. *False Consensus Effect.* Psychology. 2018. http://psychology.iresearchnet.com/social-psychology/social-cognition/false-consensus-effect/

Rosenzweig, P., *The Halo Effect ... and the Eight Other Business Delusions that Deceive Managers.* Free Press. 2007.

Ross, Lee. Greene, David. House, Pamela. *Journal Of Experimental Social Psychology*. Volume 13, Issue 3, Pages 279-301. 1977.

Rubio-Fernández, Paula., Glucksberg, Sam. *Reasoning about other people's beliefs: Bilinguals have an advantage*. Journal of Experimental Psychology: Learning, Memory, and Cognition. 38 (1): 211–217. 2012.

Schacter, Daniel L. *The Seven Sins of Memory: Insights From Psychology and Cognitive Neuroscience*. American Psychologist. 54 (3): 182–203. 1999.

Schacter, Daniel L., Gilbert, Daniel T., Wegner, Daniel M. *Psychology* (2nd ed.). Macmillan. 2011.

Sherif, M., Harvey, O.J., White, B.J., Hood, W. Sherif, C.W. *Intergroup Conflict and Cooperation: The Robbers Cave Experiment.* Norman, OK: The University Book Exchange. pp. 155–184. 1961.

Szabo, Peter, W. User Experience Mapping. Packt Publishing. 2017

Takada, T. *Self-deprecative tendencies in self-evaluation through social comparison.* Japan. J. Exp. Soc. Psychol. 27: 27–36. 1987.

Tversky, A. Kahneman, D. *Judgment under uncertainty: Heuristics and biases.* Science (New Series), 185, 1124-1131. 1974.

White, Lawrence T. Ph.D. *The Truth About "They All Look Alike to Me" Own-race bias in eyewitness identifications.* Psychology Today. 2012.

https://www.psychologytoday.com/blog/culture-conscious/201208/the-truth-about-they-all-look-alike-me

Wimmer, Heinz., Perner, Josef. *Beliefs about beliefs: Representation and constraining function of wrong beliefs in young children's understanding of deception*. Cognition. 13 (1): 103–128. 1983.

Yap, Kun-Gay. *Reality Beyond Belief: Understanding Why You Believe What You Believe*. Balboa Press. 2012.

Yoshida, Kate Shaw. *Never mind the polls—we're convinced our candidate is going to win*. Ars Technica. 2012. https://arstechnica.com/science/2012/02/in-politics-were-convinced-that-our-candidate-is-a-shoo-in/

Endnotes

[i] Ariely, Dan. Predictably Irrational. HarperCollins. 2009.

[ii] Szabo, Peter, W. User Experience Mapping. Packt Publishing. 2017

[iii] Collins, Allan, M. Loftus Elizabeth F. *A Spreading Activation Theory of Semantic Processing. Psychological Review. 82. 407-428. 10.1037//0033-295X.82.6.407. 1975.*

[iv] Brocas and Carrillo (2013)

[v] Lowenstein, and Haisley, 2008

[vi] Elder, L. Paul, R. Becoming a Critic Of Your Thinking. The Foundation for Critical Thinking. 2017. http://www.criticalthinking.org/pages/becoming-a-critic-of-your-thinking/478

[vii] Dorris, Chris. How to Develop A Disciplined Mind: Three Steps to Toughness. Chris Dorris. 2009. https://christopherdorris.com/how-to-develop-a-disciplined-mind-three-steps-to-toughness/

[viii] Pronin, E.; Kruger, J.; Savitsky, K.; Ross, L.

(2001). "You don't know me, but I know you: the illusion of asymmetric insight". Journal of Personality and Social Psychology. 81 (4): 639–656. doi:10.1037/0022-3514.81.4.639. PMID 11642351

[ix] Pronin, Emily; Matthew B. Kugler (July 2007). "Valuing thoughts, ignoring behavior: The introspection illusion as a source of the bias blind spot". Journal of Experimental Social Psychology. Elsevier. 43 (4): 565–578. doi:10.1016/j.jesp.2006.05.011. ISSN 0022-1031.

[x] Elder, L. Paul, R. Becoming a Critic Of Your Thinking. The Foundation for Critical Thinking. 2017. http://www.criticalthinking.org/pages/becoming-a-critic-of-your-thinking/478

[xi] Elder, L. Paul, R. Becoming a Critic Of Your Thinking. The Foundation for Critical Thinking. 2017. http://www.criticalthinking.org/pages/becoming-a-critic-of-your-thinking/478

[xii] Hutson, Matthew (2012). The 7 Laws of Magical Thinking: How Irrational Beliefs Keep Us Happy, Healthy, and Sane. New York: Hudson Street Press. pp. 165–81. ISBN 978-1-101-55832-4.

[xiii] Tversky, A. Kahneman, D. *Judgment under uncertainty: Heuristics and biases*. Science (New Series), 185, 1124-1131. 1974.

[xiv] Yap, Kun-Gay. *Reality Beyond Belief:*

Understanding Why You Believe What You Believe. Balboa Press. 2012.

[xv] Jenkins, Aric. Which Is Safer: Airplanes or Cars? Fortune. 2017.
http://fortune.com/2017/07/20/are-airplanes-safer-than-cars/

[xvi] Ofir, C., Raghubir, P., Brosh, G., Monroe, K. B., Heiman, A. *Memory-based store price judgments: the role of knowledge and shopping experience*. Journal of Retailing, 84(4), 414-423. 2008.

[xvii] Peer, Eyal., Gamliel, Eyal. *Heuristics and Biases in Judicial Decisions*. NCSC. 2018.
http://aja.ncsc.dni.us/publications/courtrv/cr49-2/CR49-2Peer.pdf

[xviii] Kahneman, Daniel. *Thinking, Fast And Slow*. Farrar, Straus and Giroux. 2013.

[xix] Bloom, C., Bloom, L. *The Bandwagoon Effect*. Psychology Today. 2017.
https://www.psychologytoday.com/blog/stronger-the-broken-places/201708/the-bandwagon-effect

[xx] Cassad, Bettina J. *Confirmation Bias*. Britannica. 2018.
https://www.britannica.com/topic/confirmation-bias

[xxi] Lerner, Jennifer., Tetlock, Philip. *Accounting for the Effects of Accountability*. American Psychology Association, Psychological Bulletin Vol. 125., No. 2. 225-275. 1999.

[xxi] https://scholar.harvard.edu/files/jenniferlerner/files/lerner_and_tetlock_1999_pb_paper.pdf

[xxii] Loewenstein, G. *Hot-cold empathy gaps and medical decision-making.* Health Psychology, 24(Suppl. 4), S49-S56. 2005.

[xxiii] Loewenstein, G. *Hot-cold empathy gaps and medical decision-making.* Health Psychology, 24(Suppl. 4), S49-S56. 2005.

[xxiv] Ariely, Dan. *Predictably Irrational.* Harper Collins. 2009.

[xxv] Ariely, Dan. *Predictably Irrational.* Harper Collins. 2009.

[xxvi] Gutsell, J. N. & Inzlicht, M. (2012). Intergroup differences in the sharing of emotive states: Neural evidence of an empathy gap. Social Cognitive and Affective Neuroscience, 7, 596-603.

[xxvii] Wilson, Liam. Have a Little Empathy: How to Overcome the Empathy Gap and Understand Each Other. A Cognitive Psychology Blog. 2017. https://web.colby.edu/cogblog/2017/04/17/why-cant-we-understand-each-other/

[xxviii] Stephens, J. D. W., Neal, D. S., & Overman, A. A. (2014). Closing the empathy gap in college students' judgments of end-of-life tradeoffs. International Journal of Psychology, 49(4), 313-317.

[xxix] Auyeung, K. W. & Alden, L. E. (2016). Social anxiety and empathy for social pain. Cognitive Therapy and Research, 40, 38-45.

[xxx] Nordgren, L. F., van der Pligt, J., & van Harreveld, F. (2006). Visceral drives in retrospect: Explanations about the inaccessible past. Psychological Science, 17(7), 635-640.

[xxxi] Changing Minds. *Fundamental Attribution Error.* Changing Minds. 2018. http://changingminds.org/explanations/theories/fundamental_attribution_error.htm

[xxxii] Boyes, Alice. PhD. *The Self-Serving Bias - Definition, Research, and Antidotes.* Psychology Today. 2013. https://www.psychologytoday.com/blog/in-practice/201301/the-self-serving-bias-definition-research-and-antidotes

[xxxiii] Anderson, K. B., Anderson, C. A., Dill, K. E., Deuser, W. E. *The interactive relations between trait hostility, pain and aggressive thoughts.* Aggressive Behavior, 24, 161-171. 1988.

[xxxiv] Rosenzweig, P., *The Halo Effect … and the Eight Other Business Delusions that Deceive Managers.* Free Press. 2007.

[xxxv] Kammer, D. *Differences in trait ascriptions to self and friend: Unconscious founding intensity from variability.* Psychological Reports 51, 99-102. 1982. http://psychology.wikia.com/wiki/Trait_ascription_bias

[xxxvi] McLeod, Saul. *The Milgram Experiment.* Simply Psychology. 2007.

https://www.simplypsychology.org/milgram.html

[xxxvii] Boyd, Andrew. *No. 2627 - Einstein – Bohr Debates*. The University of Houston. 2010. https://www.uh.edu/engines/epi2627.htm

[xxxviii] Psychology. *False Consensus Effect*. Psychology. 2018. http://psychology.iresearchnet.com/social-psychology/social-cognition/false-consensus-effect/

[xxxix] Ross, Lee. Greene, David. House, Pamela. *Journal Of Experimental Social Psychology*. Volume 13, Issue 3, Pages 279-301. 1977.

[xl] Hoorens, Vera. *Self-enhancement and Superiority Biases in Social Comparison*. European Review of Social Psychology. Psychology Press. 4 (1): 113–139. 1993.

[xli] Iain A. McCormick; Frank H. Walkey; Dianne E. Green (June 1986). "Comparative Perceptions of Driver Ability: A Confirmation and Expansion". Accident Analysis & Prevention. 18 (3): 205–208. doi:10.1016/0001-4575(86)90004-7.

[xlii] AAA Foundation. 2017 Traffic Safety Culture Index. AAA Foundation. 2017. http://aaafoundation.org/2017-traffic-safety-culture-index/

[xliii] Murphy, Mark. *The Dunning-Kruger Effect Shows Why Some People Think They're Great Even When Their Work Is Terrible*. Forbes. 2017. https://www.forbes.com/sites/markmurphy/201

7/01/24/the-dunning-kruger-effect-shows-why-some-people-think-theyre-great-even-when-their-work-is-terrible/#619edf465d7c

[xliv] Kendra, Cherry. *What is the Ingroup Bias?* Explore Psychology. *2016.* *https://www.explorepsychology.com/ingroup-bias/*

[xlv] Sherif, M., Harvey, O.J., White, B.J., Hood, W. Sherif, C.W. *Intergroup Conflict and Cooperation: The Robbers Cave Experiment*. Norman, OK: The University Book Exchange. pp. 155–184. 1961.

[xlvi] Changing Minds. *Context Effect.* Changing Minds. 2016. http://changingminds.org/explanations/preferences/context_effect.htm

[xlvii] White, Lawrence T. Ph.D. *The Truth About "They All Look Alike to Me" Own-race bias in eyewitness identifications.* Psychology Today. 2012. https://www.psychologytoday.com/blog/culture-conscious/201208/the-truth-about-they-all-look-alike-me

[xlviii] Kahneman, D., Tversky, A. *Evaluation by moments: Past and future.* In D. Kahneman & A. Tversky (Eds.), Choices, values and frames (pp. 2-23). New York: Cambridge University Press. 1999.

[xlix] O'Brien, Edward J., Myers, Jerome L. *When comprehension difficulty improves memory for*

text. Journal of Experimental Psychology: Learning, Memory, and Cognition. 11 (1): 12–21. 1985.

[l] Gilovich, T., Medvec, V. H., Savitsky, K. (2000). *The spotlight effect in social judgment: An egocentric bias in estimates of the salience of one's own actions and appearance.* Journal of Personality and Social Psychology, 78 (02), 211–222. 2000.

[li] Schacter, Daniel L. *The Seven Sins of Memory: Insights From Psychology and Cognitive Neuroscience.* American Psychologist. 54 (3): 182–203. 1999.

[lii] Schacter, Daniel L., Gilbert, Daniel T., Wegner, Daniel M. *Psychology* (2nd ed.). Macmillan. 2011.

[liii] Murray, Bridget. The seven sins of memory American Psychological Association. 2003.http://www.apa.org/monitor/oct03/sins.aspx

[liv] Takada, T. *Self-deprecative tendencies in self-evaluation through social comparison.* Japan. J. Exp. Soc. Psychol. 27: 27–36. 1987.

[lv] Greenberg, Jerald. *Overcoming Egocentric Bias in Perceived Fairness Through Self-Awareness.* Social Psychology Quarterly 46, no. 2, 152-56. 1983. http://www.jstor.org/stable/3033852

[lvi] Rubio-Fernández, Paula., Glucksberg, Sam. *Reasoning about other people's beliefs: Bilinguals have an advantage.* Journal of Experimental

Psychology: Learning, Memory, and Cognition. 38 (1): 211–217. 2012.

[lvii] Yoshida, Kate Shaw. *Never mind the polls—we're convinced our candidate is going to win*. Ars Technica. 2012. https://arstechnica.com/science/2012/02/in-politics-were-convinced-that-our-candidate-is-a-shoo-in/

[lviii] Whitbourne Kraus, Susan. It's a Fine Line Between Narcissism and Egocentrism. Psychology Today. 2012. https://www.psychologytoday.com/us/blog/fulfill ment-any-age/201204/it-s-fine-line-between-narcissism-and-egocentrism

[lix] Hasher, L., Goldstein, D., Toppino, T. *Frequency and the conference of referential validity*. Journal of Verbal Learning & Verbal Behaviour 16(1): 107–112. 1977.

[lx] Hasher, L., Goldstein, D., Toppino, T. *Frequency and the conference of referential validity*. Journal of Verbal Learning & Verbal Behaviour 16(1): 107–112. 1977.

[lxi] Pollage, Danielle C. *Making up History: False Memories of Fake News Stories*. Europe's Journal of Psychology. Vol. 8(2), 245–250. 2012. https://ejop.psychopen.eu/index.php/ejop/article /viewFile/456/pdf

[lxii] Fazio, Lisa K., Brashier, Nadia M., Payne, B. Keith., Marsh, Elizabeth J. *Knowledge does not*

protect against illusory truth (PDF). Journal of Experimental Psychology: General. 144 (5): 993–1002. 2015. https://web.archive.org/web/20160514233138/https://www.apa.org/pubs/journals/features/xge-0000098.pdf

[lxiii] Ellen, Scott. If you repeat a lie enough, people think it's true. Metro. 2015. https://metro.co.uk/2015/12/01/if-you-repeat-a-lie-enough-people-think-its-true-5536488/

[lxiv] Hertwig, Ralph. Gigerenzer, Gerd. Hoffrage, Ulrich. The Reiteration Effect in Hindsight Bias. Center for Adaptive Behavior and Cognition. 2001. https://www.mpib-berlin.mpg.de/volltexte/institut/dok/full/hertwig/hrreipr_/hrreipr_.html